$avvy Discount$

$avvy Discount$

The Best

Money-Saving Advice

from America's

#1 Cost-Conscious

Consumer

RICHARD deGARIS DOBLE

A Perigee Book

℗

A Perigee Book
Published by The Berkley Publishing Group
A division of Penguin Group (USA) Inc.
375 Hudson Street
New York, New York 10014

First edition: October 2003

Library of Congress Cataloging-in-Publication Data

Doble, Richard deGaris.
Savvy discounts : the best money-saving advice from America's #1 cost-conscious
consumer / by Richard deGaris Doble.
p. cm.
ISBN 0-399-52923-3
1. Consumer education. 2. Shopping. I. Title.

TX335.D62 2003
640'.73—dc21   2003042913

Printed in the United States of America

10 9 8 7 6 5 4 3 2 1

Contents

How to Use This Book

Read This First

This book, *$avvy Discount$,* could save you thousands of dollars over the next couple of years. By reading this book you will learn all the tricks to getting the very best deals. Just as important you will put the power of buying decisions back into your hands and take that power away from the salespeople, the marketing, and the hype. Here's how to get the best use of this book. No matter what products interest you, read these initial chapters:

Chapter 1: Introduction

Chapter 2: 15 Key Strategies for Saving Thousands

Chapter 3: 16 Tips to Help You Get the Very Best Deal

Chapter 11: Internet Research and Shopping, Plus Mail Order

Then read the specific chapter about a product you are considering.

Think of each chapter like a recipe: Learn about the product, comparison shop, make the best deal, be sure you got what you paid for, and then enjoy. Each chapter is divided into the following sections so that you can skim quickly and go directly to those parts that interest you the most:

Overview

What Buyers Need to Know

Comparison Shopping

Before Shopping

Buyer Beware

Discount Strategies

Making the Deal

After the Sale

Resources

Armed with this information, you can even take this book with you while you shop.
Happy shopping!

$avvy Discount$

Introduction

Getting Started on the Right Foot

This book could save you hundreds to thousands of dollars when you buy any expensive product discussed here. Buying something new, bringing it home, and making it part of your life is exciting, whether it is a new dishwasher, TV, or computer. Unfortunately, this sense of delight can often blind you to some of the things you need to do. This book asks you to step back and consider the buying process so that you will get a reliable product at the best possible price from a dealer and company that stand behind their merchandise. Now that's really exciting.

You might think that I am taking away some of the glow by encouraging you to look more closely. Salespeople and stores want you to be excited; they hope you won't drive a hard bargain. Yet nothing is more discouraging than to buy a new computer, for example, and find that you paid too much or that it does not work properly. If you have already filled out the warranty card (see my advice later in this chapter), you will have to return it to the manufacturer who can take weeks or months to repair it.

I want you to be really excited after the sale is completed, after the product is delivered, *and* after you have found that it works exactly as promised or perhaps even better. Now you can jump for joy!

The More You Know, the Better the Deal

The less you understand about a product, the more vulnerable you are to a sales pitch and to inflated claims. The more you know, the more rational you will be and less swayed by fancy listings of features and extras that are not important to you. I strongly recommend that before you start considering a buy, you surf the Internet, talk to a knowledgeable friend, and browse a couple of stores with the excuse that you are "just looking." These simple steps will also insulate you to the pressures of salespeople and keep your mind focused. In a sense you will be in training for the buying process.

Helpful Equipment and Supplies

Carry a simple notebook when you are doing serious shopping. Don't try to remember the details. If you are buying a car, for example, you might have a section for each different car model plus another for possible financing. If you are in the market for new furniture, you can use the notebook for drawings of your room where the furniture will go and measurements for the space you want to fill. Keeping a notebook has another plus: It seems to scare salespeople. If one of them says something and you write it down, suddenly the sales pressure starts to drop.

A simple filing system is also handy. You should keep and file any brochures. In addition you might get other things such as several sample swatches of cloth to show you the color and fabric that will cover your new couch. File these with a note so that you can check the color when you take delivery. After you have decided what to buy, keep the brochure about your new product since this document may have information that is not even in the manual. Throw away any other brochures for unchosen items.

Another useful tool is a digital camera or a Polaroid. For example, if you are torn between two types of exercise equipment selling at two different stores, a Polaroid will help you visualize them when you are at home and in the environment where the equipment will be placed. Polaroids are also good for documenting damage to shipping cartons or the products themselves. While you should not accept delivery of a damaged carton or item, some truckers may insist that you accept it. In that case write on the invoice a description of the possible damage and back it up with a photograph.

Technical Terms

All the purchases in this book involve technical terms and each product category has a slew of them. While it is unlikely that you will learn all the tech words, you should know the most important ones. Salespeople often gauge customers by their understanding of basic features and a classic way to manipulate a customer is to confuse him or her with a lot of technical jargon.

In addition to general product terms, each company may have its own particular name for a feature. This can lead to a lot of confusion. When talking to a salesperson, insist on using the general term because then you can compare one brand to another.

Specifications

Throughout this book I will also mention specifications. With a digital camera, for example, a specifications page on a web site (also known as the *spec sheet, technical specs* or *technical specifications*) will detail in technical terms exactly what the camera can do. It will list things such as aperture range, shutter speed range, input/output capabilities, picture resolutions, and memory. By reading the spec sheet you will familiarize yourself with many related terms and also the strengths and weaknesses of the particular model. Spec sheets are often available on the manufacturer's web site. When you come across one, print it out.

Dealing with Salespeople

You will be dealing with a salesperson when buying most products mentioned in this book. While you are probably an amateur at buying a home theater, the salespeople are pros at selling you one. It is easy for them to take advantage of you. Moreover, dealing with these people may not be relaxing. Salespeople know that once you walk out of the showroom the odds are against you coming back. The pressure is on to get you to make a decision right then and there.

I recommend that you go to several stores and compare. Hands-on comparison shopping is the best way for you to see what you are buying and what the options are. Yet when you walk into a showroom, you are fair game. Be sure you don't fall victim to the subtle psychological tactics many salespeople will use. A salesperson will try to form a bond with you and seem like a friend, and if you don't make a purchase they may become terribly disappointed in you and try to make you feel guilty.

Start out right by putting some factors in your favor. When you arrive, park far away so that the salespeople cannot see what kind of car you drive. Dress down a bit; walk slowly but deliberately and ignore the salespeople. If a salesperson starts to stay close, or follow you, keep your distance. You do not want to seem to be in a hurry. If anyone asks you if they can help, say, "I'm just looking." Don't be in a hurry to ask questions. The sales staff often divides shoppers into buyers or browsers. You want to be seen as a browser. While you are looking around, you may get a chance to judge which salesperson seems to be the most helpful and least intimidating. If you have a question, walk slowly up to that person and ask.

Bear in mind that salespeople are often not well informed about the products they sell; they only need to know a bit more than the consumer to be perceived as knowledgeable. Salespeople are in the business of selling. They are not in the business of being experts about their merchandise. The electronics industry specifically is well-known for having a sales staff that may not have a deep knowledge of the products they sell.

Because salespeople are primarily motivated by money, you should take any of their information or advice with a large grain of salt. Let them educate you about features on a particular car, but do not take their advice about which model is the best. They often recommend one model over another, because they may make more money on selected products. This is because companies often run special promotions with bonuses for the sales staff.

Be very careful about stating how much money you want to spend. Salespeople assume that if you say you have only $15,000 for a new car you will end up paying $20,000. The same holds for every item mentioned in this book. If you feel you must mention a price, use a very low figure. The assumption is that you will spend 20 percent to 40 percent more than your initial dollar amount.

Salespeople are pros when it comes to getting you to spend more than you planned. American marketing and consumerism has created such a myriad of products that there will always be one that is slightly better and more expensive. If you are going to buy a refrigerator with an ice maker, why not get one that gives you the convenience of an ice dispenser in the door without opening the fridge? While you probably don't need these extra features, it is the job of the salesperson to make you think you do.

Never state the monthly payment you can afford. With a few quick gyrations that expensive car can look affordable. The only problem is that you will be paying for it over 60 months instead of 48 and the car dealer will be earning a lot more interest.

Then there are those psychological games. Some are designed to make you defend your decision not to buy or appeal to your emotions. Some make you feel like you should follow the advice of a salesperson because you don't know enough. A salesperson might say, "You mean you didn't know that this model was the highest rated gizmo by *Consumer Reports* last year?" This sentence is designed to make you feel dumb and put the salesperson in charge. Never let yourself get talked into buying something. If you feel uncomfortable, unsure, confused, or manipulated, just don't buy it.

Now comes the moment when you want to walk out of the store and move on. This may be when you come under the most intense pressure. The sales staff won't want you to leave because they may never see you again. You may be told there is a special deal just for that day and that you had better decide quickly. This is a red flag. In this situation, my advice is simple. Leave. It is very likely that the same great bargain will be there the next day or the next week. In fact as we have pointed out there are a lot of red flags: confusing talk, a salesperson who will not leave you alone, psychological games, last-minute deals, etc. Simply put, just ignore all this, or if it gets annoying, go somewhere else.

Comparison Shopping

Comparison shopping used to mean that you went to a couple of stores and compared the price for the same or similar items. No more. Stores want to prevent you from comparison shopping. They want to make it difficult for you to compare apples to apples. Many times you will be forced to compare apples to oranges and make your best guess about how accurate your comparison really is. People in the mattress business, for example, have stated that they want to prevent comparison. So comparison shopping these days means that you have to understand the basics of mattress construction which involves springs and wire gauge. It is not all that difficult, yet probably more than you really want to know. However, armed with this simple knowledge you can accurately compare mattresses. I will go into much more detail about comparison shopping in the chapter on discount strategies.

Mission Creep

In the military you will hear the term *mission creep*. This means that you started out meaning to do one thing and found yourself much more involved than you meant to be. The same can be true when shopping.

Gone are the days of good, better, and best quality. Instead you will find slight increments in price so that virtually everyone can afford to pay just a bit more than they had budgeted for. Consumers are told that the myriad of choices is for their bene-

It's Not Exactly Bait and Switch But . . .

The old bait and switch tactic meant that when you arrived at the store for that low-cost sale item, they were always out, but instead they would sell you this much better gizmo for only a little more. With today's marketing, the low cost item is available; it's just that there are so many other tempting choices, most shoppers will end up buying a more expensive product.

fit because they can find exactly what they want. Maybe this is true. Yet it is also true that most people can be persuaded to spend a bit more, if they think that expense is justified.

Within a certain price range, the basics of a refrigerator, for example, may be the same. You might be told that a more expensive one is better made, but often it only has more features. The reason for all these choices is to get you to spend more than you planned on spending. You will find this vast array of choices with every product discussed here. For example, exercise equipment can range from under $100 for a simple exercise bicycle to over $5,000 for a treadmill, and TVs can cost less than $100 to more than $3000 for a large flat-screen high-definition model. At the web site of a major photographer retailer I counted a listing of 134 digital cameras priced from about $100 to almost $8000.

Don't Buy More Than You Need

In addition to the slight change in features and price from model to model, you may also be tempted to buy something that is really robust and expensive. While this can be a smart purchase

Is a Bigger Car Better?

I knew a man who was quite wealthy and the curator of a museum in Boston. What did he drive? A Volkswagen. I got a ride with him one day and was amazed at how easily this car could maneuver the crowded narrow backstreets of Boston. He knew all the shortcuts so we arrived in the city quickly where parking was not a problem because the car was so compact.

if you need professional industrial strength power, it is often a waste of your money. Perhaps the prime example today is the proliferation of four-wheel drive vehicles. This expensive feature is often not used by many people who own these vehicles. They have paid for a feature that does not benefit them. While large cars are all the rage today, a small car has many advantages: in a crowded city it may be easier to park; it may leave more room for storage in a home garage; it will probably get better gas mileage and cost less to begin with.

If you buy an air conditioner that is too large, the house may be freezing and then boiling. In addition a smaller AC which runs more of the time will do a better job removing humidity. A refrigerator that is too big is a waste of money, space, and energy. A half-filled fridge uses tons of electricity because there is not enough food to retain the cool temperature.

Extras, Add-Ons, Accessories, Packages

A major strategy of modern marketing is to offer a good product at a very low price because this gets you into the store. I have already covered how salespeople will try to sell you a more expensive model, but once you've bought something, the sale's pitch is not over. Let's say you buy a VCR; naturally now you will need videotape. The electronics store probably does not sell that tape at the lowest price and you may be sold a high quality, high-cost tape. Then there are tape rewinders. These are marketed to prevent wear and tear on the VCR but I have yet to see a study that shows these really save money. And of course, you might want to buy a universal remote that works with your TV, VCR, and other equipment. The more expensive the item, the more add-ons and accessories there are.

Package selling is also a big deal. Go to a furniture store to find a bed and bureau and you'll probably be shown an entire bedroom suite at what seems to be an attractive price. Try to get one or two extras on a car, and you'll find that there is a package deal that includes those and a lot more. Package selling can be a good deal if you're getting exactly what you want, but beware of being charged more for things you don't need.

Don't Buy Extended Warranties

Extended warranties are not a good idea or the best use of your money. They are really a form of high priced insurance. You will generally come out better if you pay any repair bills as they come up. The salespeople and the stores make lots of money on warranties, so you should expect the hard sell. The extended warranty generally covers repairs after the first year up to about five years. Most products fail in either the first couple of months when they are new and covered by the original warranty or when they get quite old. An extended warranty insures you during a time period when there are the fewest problems.

Extended Warranty and Bad Repair Service

I bought a large TV for my father with an extended warranty. I purchased it from a major national electronics retailer. When the TV went on the blink, the in-house authorized repair department took two months to fix it. It seemed that they were not in a hurry because we had already paid for the work.

What the salespeople are really selling is peace of mind. The assumption is that with this warranty you will not have to worry about repairs for quite some time. Don't take the bait. It is rarely a good idea to pay for something in advance. If you do need repair work, you cannot shop around for the best deal; you will have to use the service stated in the extended warranty. In my own experience, the extended warranty service from a major electronics store was not good.

K.I.S.S.

K.I.S.S. stands for "keep it simple, stupid." While the nature of technology is to get more complicated, some features work better than others. Having owned a refrigerator that had to be defrosted, I would never own one without automatic defrosting. However, some features that are fairly standard and cost a significant amount require more repair. For example, refrigerators with ice makers required a good deal more repair than those without. If you don't really need an ice maker, don't get one. You will save money and aggravation.

More expensive washers and dryers can come with push-

> **Remember, the more complicated the plumbing, the easier it is to stop up the drains!**

button electronic controls; however, these often do not work as well as the old-fashioned knobs and are expensive to fix. As a general rule you should avoid new, untested features. They may not work as advertised, are often expensive in their early development, and could require repair.

The Energy Star Label

Look for the distinctive Energy Star label for maximum energy savings on many home appliances, computers and accessories, plus audiovisual equipment. Energy Star was introduced by the U.S. Environmental Protection Agency in 1992 as a voluntary labeling program designed to identify and promote energy-efficient products. The EPA partnered with the U.S. Department of Energy in 1996 to promote the Energy Star label, with each agency taking responsibility for particular product categories. You can go to the U.S. government's Energy Star web site to look for products and stores near you that carry these efficient devices: www.energystar.gov

Return Policy

Never take the store's return policy for granted. It can vary widely. Some allow a thirty-day return, others seven or ten days. With mail order the return date may be from the date it was shipped or the date delivered. Return shipping and mandatory insurance is usually paid by the consumer and is not refundable. The initial cost of shipping and handling is not refunded either.

Restocking fees used to be common in mail order but are becoming more prevalent at other stores as well. In 2002 Target stores starting charging a restocking fee for electronics. Businesses that charge this fee will let you exchange a defective device for a new one at no charge. However, if you return an item simply because you do not like it, you can be charged a 10% or 20% restocking fee.

In all cases you will need a receipt to establish what, where, and when you bought it. File all important invoices because it is important for returns and also for any warranty repairs. If you give someone a gift, you should always include a gift receipt which will state what was bought and when but leaves out the price. This gift receipt makes returns much easier.

Also, once you have your new purchase home and unpacked, be sure to save the foam, plastic bags, boxes, and other stuff that came with it. If you must return it for a refund, you will need all of these. Later, if you ship it to the manufacturer for a repair, the company can require that you send it in the original box with the original foam protectors.

Warranties

Like the return policy, you should never take the warranty for granted. Some products are covered for a year, some for 30 days; some cover only the cost of parts, others parts and labor. When the fan on our AC went bad, I found that the five year warranty only covered the compressor but not the fan or other parts after the first year. It pays to read.

Credit Cards

For purchases around $1,000 or so, a low-interest credit card might be the best deal. Credit cards may give you certain legal rights that paying cash will not. For a valid reason, you may be able to dispute a charge on your card and not pay it while your complaint is being resolved. Since most companies are aware of the legal protection a credit card may offer, they may be more willing to settle problems. Check your credit card bill for a statement of your specific rights.

However, if you do use a credit card for a large purchase, you should decide in advance what payments you can afford. The best policy is to always pay a flat amount each month and pay more than the minimum. For example, a $1,000 computer purchase on a low-interest credit card could be paid off in less than two years with a $50 monthly payment. If you only write a check for the minimum due, you could be paying for that computer over the next ten years, long after you have traded it and bought another. In addition you might end up spending more on interest than the computer cost. Not smart!

Also, be sure to watch out for an extra charge when using a credit card. Some stores will tack on an additional amount and justify it by saying that the credit card company charges them, so they must charge the customer. Most credit card companies do not allow this practice.

The Invoice or Receipt

When appropriate, insist on a detailed itemized invoice on an official invoice form with the company's name and address printed at the top. This invoice is critical when it comes to repairs, returns, warranty questions, and legal problems. Don't be shy! Insist that anything and everything that was promised verbally be put on the invoice. Never accept abbreviations that you do not understand, instead require that they be spelled out.

Delivery

At the most exciting point in the purchasing process, the point when you take delivery of an item, you need to be the most careful and keep your guard up. Delivery is a critical point in the life of a consumer. It is the point when the company passes ownership over to you and you now own something. This can be difficult at times with a mail-order purchase because delivery people

The Subtle Point When You Take Possession

I think all of us have experienced this at some time in our lives: we go through a checkout line at a supermarket or department store only to realize that we want to return something. What would have taken only a second before checking out, now can take ten minutes and a lot of paperwork. You have become owner of the item, so returning it means that you must have a receipt, probably sign a form, and then sign a credit receipt before you can get your money back.

Taking delivery is an almost invisible, but critical point. If you are not satisfied, if the shipper or company has not lived up to its agreement, refuse the item as long as you can document that the agreement was broken. Once you have accepted delivery, you will have a much harder time getting satisfaction and have much less leverage with the company.

just want to drop off an item, get you to sign for it, and go on their merry way. But wait! You really need to inspect the package for any damage, and be certain you got the make and model you ordered. Before signing the receipt inspect all the merchandise. Once you have taken delivery, problems may have to be solved by you.

Warranty Cards

You *should not fill out the warranty card* until the time to return the product for a refund or exchange has passed. Most people are very surprised by this advice. Once you fill out that card, you are dealing with the manufacturer not the store. Got a problem? After filling out the card, you'll have to send it back postpaid and insured to get it fixed. This could take several weeks. If you hadn't filled out the card, you could go back to the store and demand another one or get a refund. In short you could be stuck with a lemon.

What you must have and must keep is the invoice. The invoice proves where and when you bought the product. The invoice is more important than the warranty card. The warranty card is really used to ask a lot of personal questions so that companies can get a free survey about who uses their merchandise. If you do fill out the card, you do not have to answer anything more than basic information such as your name, address, and the store where you bought it.

There are good reasons for filling out a warranty card *after* the time to return it to the store has passed. Sending in the card means that you will be notified of recalls, for example. If you don't send it, the company won't know how to get in touch with you.

The First Few Days Run It Through Its Paces

Most problems with a product show up in the first couple days. But you must give it a full workout. Try out all the features; tweak all the dials; check that it is doing what it is supposed to be doing. When you set the new washing machine on hot, is the water hot or just lukewarm? Try all the adjustments on your new exercise bicycle. With electronic goods you should test all of the capabilities plus leave the device on constantly for at least 24 hours. If your new gizmo passes these initial tests, it will probably work well for years.

In a sense, the product you just bought is on probation. It belongs to you, but only if it behaves and does what it's told. Otherwise you can return it for a refund or exchange. Going through this "get acquainted" process means that you will feel more comfortable with the new gizmo and be aware of what it can do. There is an additional advantage as well: you might ac-

Can a New Computer End Up in the Shop for Months?

Think this can't happen? I get e-mails all the time about this situation. For example, one young man sent his computer back to the manufacturer several times to be fixed and it still didn't work properly. For months he was getting the runaround; no one would take responsibility, clearly he had a lemon and it needed to be exchanged, but he could not find anyone at the company who would do this. If he had not filled out the warranty card, but simply returned the computer to the store, he could have resolved the problem quickly.

tually learn how to program your VCR if you read the instruction book and press the right buttons.

Read the Manual

Although it goes against the American character, you should really read the manual. Just about every product in this book will have a manual with important information. In fact there might be a booklet plus additional loose sheets with important notices. As things get more complicated and high-tech, there will be a greater need for the consumer to understand the capabilities and limitations of manufactured products. For example, a digital camera may have several methods for transferring files from the camera to the computer. One method may work a lot better for one system than another. Yet only by reading the manual will you be able to understand the options open to you.

Why You Should Read the Manual

A friend of mine owned a digital camera for years. He used it constantly, but like most of us had only glanced at the manual. One day, I was taking a picture with his camera, and I continued to hold the shutter button down after taking the photo which meant the new image displayed on the back. "I didn't know you could do that," he exclaimed. He had been going through the painstaking process of switching back and forth between Camera mode and Display mode, yet this was explained clearly in the manual.

Save All Those Boxes—Be Organized

Since we own more and more "stuff," we also collect and need to organize more and more invoices, guarantees, etc. I suggest that you have one place where you file all of the following:

—Notes that you took when you made the order

—The invoice or receipt when you bought the product

—The booklet, manual, or info sheets that came with the product

You might want to divide this filing system into two parts: one for the really expensive items like a car or dishwasher and a second one for less expensive items such as a microwave or a toaster.

Getting a Refund

If you do need to return a product for a refund, make sure that you get all the money you are due. While shipping and handling is often not refunded with mail order, sales tax should be. In addition, make sure that you are refunded the money that you paid. If an item has gone on sale since you bought it, some stores try to refund only the current sale price, not the money you actually forked over. Don't accept this. Bring your receipt with you or make a copy; circle the item and the price you paid on the duplicate and demand a refund of the entire amount you paid.

Exchange

If you think that your product is not working as advertised, you should be able to exchange it for another one at the place where you bought it within the time period allowed for exchanges. Most stores will be glad to exchange a faulty product, even mail-order companies. Stores that charge restocking fees should not charge for an exchange. As always, bring the receipt, or mail a copy if you are exchanging with a mail-order firm.

What is a Lemon?

While generally applied to the car business, a lemon really applies to all products. If you buy a new item that breaks and after being repaired keeps breaking, you should ask the manufacturer to replace it. The rule of thumb is that after about three repairs you should get a replacement. While the company may not be legally obligated to do this, the mention of the word *lemon* might just get someone's attention.

15 Key Strategies for Saving Thousands

Or Doesn't This Go on Sale Soon?

Overview

We will go into detail about each strategy but here is an overview of the strategies that could save you thousands over the years. You are not limited to using just one strategy at a time; often you can combine two, three, or even more strategies to get the very best price. I will explain how to do this at the end of the chapter.

1. Comparison shopping

2. Haggling for a low price

3. Haggling for extras

4. Custom configurations

5. Regular sales

6. Rebates

7. Unusual discounts and sales

8. Internet shopping and mail order

9. Outlet stores and outlet malls

10. Closeouts and discontinued models

11. Floor models, demonstrators, scratch-and-dent blemished, seconds

12. Refurbished

13. Used

14. Financing

15. Extra discounts

Strategies in Detail

1. Comparison shopping

Comparison shopping is essential and the most important of these fifteen strategies. In fact, to get the most out of all these tactics, you will need to have compared products and prices. Comparison shopping does not simply mean that you go to a couple of stores and find that a product sells for $300 at one store, $275 at another, and $350 at a third. In today's sophisticated economy of manufacturing and marketing you may find that straightforward across-the-board comparisons can be quite difficult. There are generally two reasons for this.

Reason One: Different manufacturers offer different features. Ideally you might want to combine the features offered by two companies, but that is impossible. So you will need to decide what features are most important and what features you can live without.

Reason Two: Products are often designed to confuse you and manufactured to make comparison difficult. Mattresses are a perfect example—different stores may carry virtually the same mattress but with a different model name, making them difficult to compare.

So how do you cut through all this garble and decide what is the best deal at the best price? I suggest that you do your research and take your time before making a buying decision. The more money you plan to spend, the more time you should take. Believe me, you will be paid back handsomely with a reliable product that will last for years and that will cost you a lot less.

You will need to investigate the various makes, models, and prices. You must grab brochures, take notes, and ask questions. Even after all this there's a good chance you will still be thoroughly confused, but don't worry; there are several ways to sort through your confusion. You should be able to find real repair history information (large statistical summaries) about each product. There is a wealth of repair history information about cars and major appliances.

Also take into consideration any extra cost and time involved. With large items like exercise equipment, appliances, and furniture, you don't simply buy the product, it must be delivered, installed or assembled, and you might have to remove your old one. These services usually come with a price tag, not to mention a lot of waiting around for the delivery truck. Make sure that you include this when you compare several products as a company that charges a bit more for a refrigerator, but has a good price and service for delivery might be a better deal than a discount warehouse that simply plops the fridge on your doorstep and drives away.

This comparison of extra or additional charges even applies

to mail-order and smaller items. For example, I found that many companies that charged the lowest prices on the Internet also charged a lot for shipping.

But wait! There is still more to be said about comparison shopping. As I said in the Introduction, in today's market you will often be overwhelmed by the number of choices. At a discount home repair and appliance store, I counted thirty-nine full-sized refrigerators that ranged in price from about $400 to over $1700. That's quite a range. The difference in price between one model and the next was often a very affordable $30. So for just a little bit more . . .

Before you are ready to open your wallet and buy, you should decide on the features you must have and the maximum price you will pay. Otherwise you will be at the mercy of a slick salesperson who will try to up sell you the next pricier model. In addition you need to consider the cost of owning, running, and keeping the product. Don't just compare one refrigerator to another; compare the operating cost with the EnergyGuide sticker, which must be posted on the outside of all new models. Miles per gallon information must be posted on all new cars.

A digital camera, for example, generally costs more than a traditional one. You will not need to buy film, or drop it off at the local drugstore or pay for a full set of prints. You will, however, need more storage space in your computer and perhaps a new printer and new software to print your photographs. Some air conditioners are much more efficient than others and will cost less to run. Some new refrigerators use only about as much electricity as a lightbulb. Different new cars, even in the same price range and with the same gas mileage, may have different collision insurance costs.

When you compare prices, you should estimate these for the

life of the item; then add them to the purchase price for a complete overview and a realistic comparison.

Maintenance is another important consideration. For example, a window air conditioner with an easy to pull out filter will save you money in the long run, because cleaning a filter is the most important way to save money on cooling costs and keep your AC in top running condition. Jewelry may need to be reset; exercise equipment will wear over time.

At this point, in your notebook, you should have a list of the makes, models, sizes, and colors that you are considering, along with the cost and other considerations such as delivery and assembly. Next make a list of features that you must have and a list of features that might be nice, and you should have a realistic listing of products, features, models, operating costs, maintenance, delivery, installation, and prices.

When you are able to compare prices directly, that is model for model, you will often find some big differences. In one report, virtually the same mattress sold for as low as $600 or as high as $1500. Just a little Internet browsing should save you an easy 10% or more from established reputable dealers.

Doing all this comparing has an additional benefit. You will not only have gained an understanding of what things cost, you will also have gained a knowledge of how products work and what you will need to do to keep them in like-new condition.

2. Haggling for a low price

All that comparison shopping you did will now pay off. Since you have done your homework, you are armed and dangerous. You can walk into a store and say, "I can get an Alpha Brand with the same features and a great repair record for $50 less than your Beta brand. Can you match that price?" In a sense you have leveled the playing field between you and the salesperson, because you now know as much, perhaps more, than they do.

Many stores expect you to bargain, especially when it comes to cars, appliances, mattresses, and furniture. In addition, you can bargain during seasonal sales and on discontinued, floor, or scratch-and-dent models. You should always haggle over the price of a used product. Experts believe that you can save 10 to 20 percent right off the bat. If you are not experienced at bargaining, you might start with these simple phrases, "Would you take less for this?" or "What is the lowest price you would sell this for?" If you buy several expensive items, you should ask for an extra 5 to 10 percent off. Consider it a volume discount.

There are times when businesses are more willing to bargain than others. You might be in a better position just before inventory or at the end of a month when a salesperson has to fill his or her quota. This is often the case with automobiles.

SPECIAL NOTE:

A number of surveys have found that women pay more for cars and other items when haggling. The salesperson begins with a higher figure than that for men and even after the bargaining process does not come down as far as the lowest figure offered to men. What is a woman to do? I believe that a woman can calculate a reasonable figure for the price of a new car using the resources listed at the end of the chapter on automobiles. She can then make an offer based on her math. She should show the dealer how she arrived at that figure. If the dealer will not budge from a higher figure, she should mention that she had heard women usually paid more than men for the same vehicle. At this point I believe the dealer will agree to a lower price.

3. Haggling for extras

Haggling can take different forms. If you are a loyal customer of a furniture or appliance store, remind the owners that you continue to shop at their store instead of at the new competing national chain warehouse. Then ask them to throw in the delivery for free. I have discovered that for accounting reasons, many stores are often more willing to give you a free delivery and/or setup, worth $100, than give you a discount of $100 on the product. So if you cannot get a store to budge on its price, ask the salesperson to throw in the delivery for nothing. You can also ask to get an accessory for free. In a sense you are turning the table on the sales staff. Instead of their suggesting that you buy a bunch of extras, you instead propose that they give you some extras as a bonus.

4. Custom configurations

Some products lend themselves to custom designs and if such a design will save you money, why not? If you are knowledgeable,

An Estimate is Not a Quote a Quote is Not an Estimate

If you want a custom-made product, you will need to get an estimate or a quote for the work to be done. A friend who runs a large factory taught me this important distinction: an estimate is just what it says, a rough idea; a quote is very specific. Expect an estimate to always go higher. However, if you are quoted a price in writing, the company must stick to that unless something totally out-of-the-ordinary occurs. Even so, the company should involve you with any revision of that quote.

you can have it tailored to your exact specifications. For example, a computer built just for your needs is often the best buy. You will not be paying for hardware and software that you don't need. This same useless stuff will not be interfering with the software and hardware that you do use. You can also have devices and features added that are not normally available. This can also be the case with exercise equipment: You can create your own custom exercise workout center rather than buying an entire home gym from one company. A component stereo system can also be a much better deal than an all-in-one setup if you understand how to put a system together.

5. Regular sales

Most products go on sale on a regular basis. We have included a calendar at the end of this chapter showing generally when products mentioned in this book will be discounted year after year. Most products are seasonal. Buying off-season is a good time to get a great deal. However, if you wait too long, you may find that the items are sold out or there is a poor selection. Buying an air conditioner in December might be difficult. The main sales will be before the season has begun and after it has ended. Generally, you will find the best selection before the season, but the price may be a bit higher too.

6. Rebates

Rebates seem like a really good idea. They seem like a sale, but they are quite different. A rebate is not a true discount; it is a promise of cash back if you meet certain conditions. In addition you will pay taxes on the full price, not the cost after the rebate.

The main problem with rebates is the "terms and conditions." In order to take advantage you must carefully follow a long list of rules. These are often hard to understand, there is little or no customer support, and many times the rules are contradictory. All rebates have a deadline and a substantial number of people never send them. According to the *Wall Street Journal* (6/11/02), only 40% of rebates for expensive electronic items were mailed. Even so, about 20% of these forms were rejected. Bottom line: Never buy a product just because of the rebate.

Nevertheless, you can find substantial rebates on computers, audiovisual equipment, cars, and appliances. If the rebate is large enough, it might be worth the hassle. I recommend that you avoid rebates for less than $50. If you find an attractive rebate, read the terms and conditions on the form first. These spell out exactly what documentation is needed, in what form, and when.

If you do buy with a rebate in mind, I recommend that you get a separate receipt for that particular item when you check out. This simply means you don't lump the purchase of the rebate item with other things. This makes it much easier to keep track of the receipt: If you must send in the entire original receipt, you will not lose the paperwork for the other items that were purchased at the same time. Write down on a calendar the deadline for mailing the rebate. Make sure that you follow each rule exactly and mail it at least ten days ahead of time. In addition you should keep copies of all materials that you mail, including the form, just in case your rebate is denied.

7. Unusual discounts and sales

In a difficult economy or when a company has overproduced products (known as overstocks), or when fashions change, you may find sales on cars, furniture, audiovisual equipment, and computers. If you are sensitive to changes in the economy and watch the evening news, you can pretty well predict what will go on sale. For example, when home sales are booming, goods associated with new homes tend to sell at a premium. When home sales are slumping, you can expect to find substantial discounts on furniture.

In the fall of 2002, a major electronics store was offering zero percent financing for TVs, stereos, home theaters, and camcorders. They did this because the economy had slowed down and they wanted to boost sales leading into Christmas. Many Internet and mail-order businesses were also offering free shipping in this same time period.

Office supply stores may offer free shipping for orders over a minimum amount. They carry many of the products listed in this book, such as computers and peripherals, plus digital cameras and ready-to-assemble furniture.

In order to attract business, some Internet companies offer discounts or free shipping only if you order directly from the site.

Oddly, a downward turn in the economy can send the price of some items higher. When no one can afford to buy a new car, you may find that the price of used cars has gone up significantly. In this case, you would do well to investigate the prices of new cars as well as used. When new cars are selling well, the price of used cars tends to drop because the dealer now has to get rid of all those trade-ins.

8. Internet shopping and mail order

I have bought much of my photography and computer equipment through the mail. The selection is simply the best. Now with the Internet, comparison shopping is not all that difficult. Please go to the chapter on Internet Research and Shopping, Plus Mail Order to read more about comparing prices on the Web and ordering at a distance.

I often find a 10% difference between the listed prices of

new things, meaning that a little Web surfing can easily save me $100 on a $1,000 item. In addition to new products, you can now find used items via eBay, and refurbished items at manufacturers' sites. Always check recent sales on eBay to find what something has sold for in the last couple of months before placing a bid at a current auction. Naturally you need to consider more than just price. The reputation of the store, the shipping and handling, and the return policy are all important.

9. Outlet stores and outlet malls

Because outlets sell directly to the customer and skip the middleman, you can expect lower prices. There are hundreds of outlet centers across the U.S.A. If you know of one near you, you should check it out. However, it's not always smart to buy an expensive product from a store that is a day's drive away. If you have problems, it will not be easy to return.

You can get a directory of about 14,000 outlets in the U.S.A. and Canada from outletbound.com. You can search by location, store, brand, or category.

There are also quite a few online factory outlets where you may find a variety of discounted new products. Large manufacturers often have their own online factory outlets. Check their web sites.

10. Closeouts and discontinued models

Do not be afraid of models that are no longer being made. There is a saying in some industries that "all models are discontinued eventually." They should come with the same guarantee as a new model. If they do not, you should negotiate an even lower discount.

A business is highly motivated to get rid of a discontinued model because soon it will have the appearance of being old and

COSMETIC BLEMISH CUTS PRICE 50%

A friend of mine bought a top of the line amplifier some years ago because the company's emblem had been put upside down on the unit. Talk about a deal. He got it for 50% off, no one ever noticed the emblem, and it certainly sounded fine!

out of fashion. Major manufacturers are selling these directly over the Internet. Check their web sites.

11. Floor models, demonstrators, scratch-and-dent, blemished, seconds

Do not be afraid of these as long as they come with a full manufacturer's guarantee. While floor models may look a bit used, you should think of them as being thoroughly tested. Since they are floor models, you can run them through their paces right there in the store. With a digital camera, for example, you could take a few pictures and judge the quality.

Remember that all those dozens of TVs you see on display at an electronics store may eventually become floor models that must be sold for a song. Always ask to see these before looking at new ones.

12. Refurbished

Refurbished can go by a number of names including reconditioned, factory serviced, and rebuilt, but it all means the same thing; a new product was returned to the manufacturer who had the device repaired and tested before reselling it.

Refurbished electronics such as computers and audiovisual

equipment can be a really good deal. New equipment as it comes off the production line is often only spot checked. This means that the latest model TV you bought has probably never been thoroughly tested. However, a refurbished electronic item has been thoroughly looked at. This makes it, in a sense, a better deal even at the same price, yet refurbished items often sell for 30% off.

Many major companies may sell refurbished products and equipment directly from their web site. Hewlett-Packard, for example, has an online factory outlet where you can choose from a number of refurbished items. A search on the Internet for "refurbished outlets" and add the product name will bring up a number of companies that sell refurbished merchandise. As always, never buy without reading the fine print and checking out the company's reputation. Look for businesses that have a physical address, have been in business for a number of years, and have had few complaints lodged against them.

With refurbished items, it is especially important to look at the warranty. Try to get the same warranty you would get buying new. If not, this is one case where an extended warranty might be a good idea. Buy one that will keep your refurbished product under warranty for as long as a new product.

13. Used

Buying quality used merchandise generally will give you the biggest discount of all the strategies listed here. Like-new exercise equipment can sell for 75% off the original price. A four-year-old car might sell at 50% less than the new price. Used makes a lot of sense when buying a car, some furniture, and exercise equipment because the savings can be dramatic. Solid furniture in good condition can go for almost nothing at a yard sale or a consignment shop.

If you only need a computer to do simple word processing, spreadsheets, and database work, you might locate an older reliable machine for practically nothing. However, you should not buy antique or used jewelry unless you really know what you are doing. It is easy to be fooled. I also think that new major appliances will generally be more efficient and last much longer than used. I don't think there is any real advantage to buying audiovisual equipment used unless you find a fantastic deal.

You will find a wide variety of used equipment on the Internet such as at eBay. Since most used items do not come with a warranty, you must be very careful to buy from reliable dealers. I would not purchase over the Internet unless you can return the item for a full refund. Look for businesses that have a physical address, have been in business for a number of years, and have had few complaints lodged against them. eBay has a rating for each dealer and keeps a log of comments from buyers. You should read these before making a bid.

14. Financing

Don't get a great deal and then blow the financing which can double your price. In-store financing is often over 20%.

When buying a car, shop around for the best loan on a new or used car. If you are buying a large amount of furniture, you might be able to get bank financing.

Some credit cards have a 10% or less interest rate. If you qualify for one of these, this might be a smart way to finance your purchase under $1,000. However, in this case, do not just pay the minimum, but instead discipline yourself to pay a set amount every month so that the loan is paid off in a couple of years instead of over a decade, which is what will happen if you only pay the minimum.

When you see a good financing deal such as "no payments or interest for six months" read the fine print. Some of these deals are quite tricky with serious penalties and high interest if you do not pay on time when payments are required.

Some stores advertise that 90 days is the same as cash meaning that if you pay the full amount within 90 days, there will be no interest charge. If you plan to use this option, do not mention it until you have negotiated your final price. At this point you can say that you want to take advantage of the "90 days same as cash" promotion. I recommend that you bring a copy of the ad with you.

Also since an offer of free financing for a year does cost the store money, you should get a discount if you offer to pay cash. For example, I received an offer in the mail for zero payments and interest for six months from a home-improvement store. If I bought $1000 worth of products and paid cash, I could negotiate a further price reduction. Since the entire amount of $1,000 would be financed for six months and the store interest is generally around 20% per year or 10% for six months, it will cost the store about $100 ($1,000 × 10%). Therefore, I would ask the store for a $100 discount for paying cash.

15. Extra discounts

There is no such thing as a free lunch! If you are buying an expensive folding bed, the company might give you a free TV as a promotion. If you don't need the TV, ask for a discount. Why get and pay for a TV you don't need? Computers often come with free printers or scanners. Again if you don't need it, don't pay for it even though it is being presented as free. Package deals are often represented as giving you free accessories. Yet the retailer has added the price of the "free" things into the overall price. If you don't need those extras, say so and request a better deal. Remember nothing is free. Instead, take the money.

Another extra discount comes from owning a stock. Some companies, such as IBM, give discounts to their stockholders. Just owning one share could entitle you to substantial savings at a number of companies.

Combining Discounts

Combining discounts will give you the most bang for the buck. This is not hard to do. Here is an example of three discounts on one product.

Example of a Combined Discount

I bought a Casio digital camera from a large national chain office supply store for $50 when the list price was about $300. In addition the store threw in an AC power cord, which meant I could save a substantial amount of money on batteries. There were a few reasons I got such a low price; the camera was a floor model and it was being discontinued, and a couple of unimportant items were missing from the package, things like a cleaning cloth. I knew these things were missing because I had gone to the manufacturer's web site and found a list of what was in the box when it was shipped from the factory. I printed this and took it with me to the store.

The store was more than willing to negotiate with me. At first they wanted $100 but settled for $50. I got the full normal warranty. Six years later, the camera is still working and I still use it.

At the end of the season (first discount) you find a discontinued model (second discount) that is slightly dinged up (third discount). You are in a position to negotiate a fantastic deal. The seller will be highly motivated to get rid of this product, because he or she does not want it around the following year. Let's say that an end-of-season sale might get you a 10% discount, a discontinued model another 15% discount, and a scratch-and-dent a further 20% off. When you add these together, you should expect about a 45% discount from the normal selling price.

Regular Sales Months

These are the months when you will typically (but not always or in all areas) find sales on the items mentioned in this book.

January: Appliances, furniture.

February: Air conditioners, audiovisual equipment, computers, exercise equipment, furniture, mattresses, used cars. Look for special sales around President's Day.

March: Laundry appliances.

April: No regular sales.

May: Jewelry, outdoor furniture, TVs.

June: Furniture, mattresses.

July: Air conditioners, appliances, audiovisual equipment, furniture.

August: Furniture.

September: New cars from the current year model after the new model introduction of next year's models (NMI), furniture. Look for special Labor Day sales.

October: Appliances, new cars from the current year model after the new model introduction of next year's models (NMI).

November: Appliances, used cars.

December: Don't buy anything around Christmas.

Tips for Spotting Genuine Discounts and Sales

When a store claims to be having a sale, how do you know that you are getting a genuine discount? Do you know the difference between a sale item and a closeout? Read the following to understand what these discounts really involve.

WHAT IS A SALE?

The word *sale* has a specific legal meaning. A sale is a temporary markdown or a special promotion; the price will go back to the regular price after the sale is over. A sale must offer a real discount, that is items not usually selling at that price. Some stores have sales so often the government has ruled that they are not really sales, but rather the normal price. The terms *clearance* or *closeout* mean the price will not go back up. After a clearance sale, the price only goes down further and the items may eventually be thrown out, put on a bargain table, or given to a charity.

BOGUS WORDS:

The following words and phrases sound good but have no real legal meaning: *special, unusual, extraordinary, special value* or *purchase, special buy, value pack, priced right.*

38

"REGULAR" AND "ORIGINAL" PRICE:

Beware of inflated discounts! As I point out, jewelry seems to go for half price just when the demand is the greatest, such as before Christmas or Valentine's Day. I would be very suspicious of the regular price. Listen to what the Federal Trade Commission says about this practice, "If . . . the former price being advertised is not bona fide but fictitious—for example, where an artificial, inflated price was established for the purpose of enabling the subsequent offer of a large reduction—the 'bargain' being advertised is a false one; the purchaser is not receiving the unusual value he expects. In such a case, the 'reduced' price is, in reality, probably just the seller's regular price." To read more at the FTC site about this and other deceptive practices, go to: www.ftc.gov

WILL THIS EVER GO ON SALE?

If you ask, a salesperson may tell you if and when the computer or stereo you want will go on sale. Here are some questions you might ask. Will this go on sale soon or in the next year? Has this ever gone on sale? When? What else will go on sale or has gone on sale? Some stores will even let you buy something today and get money back later when it goes on sale—usually within a month. For example, when I bought my first computer for $400, I asked if it ever went on sale. I was told it would go on sale in two weeks for $300 and that I could bring back my receipt and get a $100 refund.

TAKE THE AD WITH YOU:

When you see an advertisement in the newspaper for a great sale, or you get a circular in the mail, take the ad with you to the store. Several times I've gone to take advantage of a sale, but no one in the store knew what I was talking about. When you bring the ad, they are under a legal obligation to honor the offer.

GET ON MAILING LISTS:

At a department store or web site ask to be placed on a department's "preferred customer list" so they will contact you prior to a sale.

GET ON E-MAIL LISTS:

A number of online companies will notify you of closeouts, overstocks, and refurbished sales. Dell Computer, for example, has a closeout and sale newsletter.

Other Tips

Smaller local stores often have more flexibility than larger chain stores to bargain with you, yet one of my best deals was from a major chain office supply store. Once a store has cut the original set price for an item, you can haggle. By discounting the normal price, the store has indicated that it is willing to deal. While a clerk may not have the authority to bargain with you, the manager often does. This does not always work, but you might be surprised.

Before you start drooling over new merchandise, ask to see any discontinued models, scratch-and-dent, and floor models.

Understanding How Businesses Operate

There is a saying where I live on the coast of North Carolina, "If you want to catch fish, you have to think like a fish." The same goes for getting a deal from a business: If you want to haggle with a business, think like a business. When or under what conditions will the business be most likely to give you a good discount?

Often, what you see first will be what you buy, so if you look at the inexpensive stuff first, you are more likely to purchase that.

Grand openings are often a great way to get a really great deal. Why? This flashy opening is for publicity as much as sales. The company wants to get new customers into the store so they will start shopping there, and the business wants to create goodwill.

Lowest Price Guaranteed?

What about that "lowest price" guarantee that many stores offer? How about the ones that will refund the difference plus 10% if you find a lower price? Consider this to be a marketing tactic. The purpose of this guarantee is to get you to avoid comparison shopping. The policy is designed to set your mind at ease. But, you say, the store must have the lowest prices or they wouldn't offer this guarantee—right? Wrong!

There are two reasons why this guarantee is almost meaningless. First of all, you must locate the same model number to get that refund and some manufacturers make unique models for large superstores—this means you will not be able to find that model anywhere else. Second, who is going to do a lot of comparison shopping for the same model after they have already bought something? Not very many people.

In brief do your comparison shopping first and don't trust the word of the store that you are getting a rock-bottom price.

Watch Out for These Price Premiums

You can find yourself in situations where you must pay top dollar and discounts are hard to come by. Here are some things to avoid.

A good rule of thumb is never to buy anything close to Christmas. This is the one time of year most retailers can charge full price and not haggle with you. They know that you have a deadline; it's December 25. Many stores make as much as half of their income during the two months of November and December.

Recently, rebates have become popular around Christmastime. For example, the price of the product in advertisements and at the store might be listed as "only $100 after $100 rebate." This means that you will pay $200 for the item. Maybe you will remember to mail in the rebate during the busy holiday season and maybe you won't. Manufacturers expect that many people will never send in the form. You may occasionally find good deals in December, but they are few and far between. Save your money for January when stores are really desperate.

It is unlikely that you will be able to do much haggling over the price of a popular car model that is back ordered at the factory. At this point you should go to your second choice.

Finally, avoid buying any product at peak season when demand is high.

Special Note: Why Businesses Discount Products and When

Why do businesses discount products at some times of the year and not others? Will a business sell something to you below cost?

While businesses know a lot about consumer psychology, you can level the playing field a bit by understanding business psychology. When, for example, will a business be most willing to haggle with you?

To state the obvious, businesses are there to make a profit. Yet they do not have to make a huge profit on every sale. When they look at the bottom line of all sales, they want to see a profit. However, there are times when they might even sell something at cost or below. It is up to you, the consumer, to know when you can take advantage. Any business may sell an item at a loss if it cannot be returned, is slightly damaged, or does not invite customer interest. It is better for the business to get rid of this item at any cost. It can then use the money from that sale to buy other items that will move. So now you know how I bought the digital camera for $50 from a major office supply store. Read more about this in the section on combined discounts in this chapter.

16 Tips to Help You Get the Very Best Deal

Savvy Advice from a Seasoned Shopper

1. Features, Features, Features

The modern trend is to add more features to any product. Even furniture can come with extras, such as reclining chairs with vibrators or trays. The joke goes that people with Masters degrees cannot program their VCRs. Just because a device has a feature does not mean you will use it. While you will often have to buy a model with more features than you want, don't pay extra for things you may never use. Adding features should not interfere with the basic operation. Even a state-of-the-art phone with a speaker, memory, and speed dialing should be simple if you just want to make a call.

Some features are well worth it. I found that the electronic ignition on our gas stove used much less gas than the old pilot design and the kitchen was cooler in the summer. A dishwasher with a temperature boost will save you money on your hot water bill. You'll be able to turn the water heater setting down and still get very hot temperatures to clean the dishes.

2. Don't Be the First on Your Block to Own the Latest and Greatest

While you might be the envy of your neighbors for a few weeks, you'll cry all the way to the bank. Why? The latest model of anything technological is bound to have bugs in it. This goes for computers, appliances, electronics, you name it. The more complicated, the more careful you should be. The first products are often expensive, bulky or heavy, and not completely thought out. Wait a few years and get a much better deal. Instead, buy something that has been thoroughly tested and has proven itself. In the case of a new device, you might want to wait to buy it in the second year of production.

I've seen ads for $2,000 home-theater entertainment units promising that they are upgradeable in the future to high-definition television (HDTV). I have to be skeptical. In any case, why invite the hassles of repair shops, complaint letters, and lemon laws? Buying a tried and true device is a no-brainer.

Years ago, I learned this lesson the hard way. As a starving university student, I scraped together enough money to buy a new professional camera. It was an early production model of a new design. Just about everything that could go wrong did. Although the company repaired it for free, the camera spent half its time in the shop. Some things that were fixed broke down again. Now that I know better, I would have insisted that the company recognize this as a lemon and replace it completely.

3. Think Modular

You may have to choose between buying two or more devices and a combination such as a TV-VCR. When there is very little price difference and it is not inconvenient, I always recommend going modular. Why? With the TV-VCR, if either one breaks down, you will have to take the entire unit to the repair shop.

Sometimes a combo does make sense, such as a $100 boom box with everything built in. It is convenient to carry around while several modular pieces would be clumsy.

4. Flexibility

A flexible product will give you many more choices about how it is to be used. A boom box with a full set of places to plug in is usually not expensive and much more useful. It gives you the option of attaching an extra device such as a microphone or keyboard.

A kitchen cart on casters can be positioned where you need it. An exercise machine that collapses out of the way will give you more space.

My external ZIP® drive for my old computer works just as well with my new computer. All I do is plug it into the USB port in the back. If the ZIP® drive had been built in, I would have lost that money and also the ability to plug the drive into the several computers that I use.

5. Think Design

A good design is a joy. It is simple, straightforward, and a no-brainer. Think of the telephone, it is so easy to use we don't even notice it.

A good design never leaves you guessing. A solid click tells you that a knob has been turned on or off. A clear error message means something went wrong. The steps involved are almost intuitive. A good design often fits well in your hands and clearly displays its controls. Avoid confusing or awkward designs.

6. Are You Asking the Right Questions?

People often call me and say, "Hey, Rick, I need a computer. What should I get?" My immediate response is not what they expect. I reply, "Before I can answer that, what do you need your computer to do?" As the CEO of Black and Decker has pointed out, "People don't want ¼-inch drills, they want ¼-inch holes."

How often have we all bought something because we thought we might use it and never did? If you simply want to balance your checkbook, a computer might be overkill. I recommend buying technology only when you have a specific and urgent need to accomplish a task.

7. Cheaper, Better, Smaller, Lighter

Technology and electronics, in particular, tend to get much cheaper over time. Consider these examples: The first low-priced consumer VCRs cost $1,000 around 1980. They were large and had few controls. The first microwaves were expensive and monsters. Refrigerators were the same. The price of computers keeps dropping by about 50% every two years. Cell phones are getting better and cheaper. Unless you have a crying need for something, wait. You have nothing to lose.

48

Today the Hewlett Packard laser printer is the standard in laser black-and-white printing. Mine has worked flawlessly for over five years, but if I do have any problems, I can get it fixed. All my software knows how to work with it. I could even sell it for a good price.

8. Buy the Industry Standard When Possible

As a photographer I learned that my life was much easier if I bought standard cameras and slide projectors than if I tried odd-ball stuff. A device becomes a standard for a reason. It is usually a better or more durable design. In addition, a standard means that you can find parts easily and technicians who understand how to do repairs. If you need to, you can sell a standard product in a heartbeat. Wherever you travel, people will know how to use it.

9. Standards Are Changing

Major standards will be changing soon. Some of these have been mandated by the government, such as the switch from conventional TV to high-definition TV (HDTV), and others seem inevitable, such as the evolution from film-based to digital photography. There are also these important standards that are gaining ground: MP3, DVD, digital audiocassette, and digital video.

Since technology is always changing, this should not stop you from buying what you need, but it should be a factor that you take into consideration. Before you invest major bucks in a serious film-based photography system you should consider where photography is headed. As a professional photographer, I believe that digital is the wave of the future but that we have a number of years to go before it is worked out. I would not recommend buying an expensive full-fledged film-based camera with inter-changeable lenses unless you absolutely need it right now.

49

10. Trust Your Own Eyes, Not the Reviews

Just because you have read a glowing review does not mean the product is right for you. Other designs may have a loyal following. In any case, you are the final authority, and you will have to pay for and live with what you buy.

11. Brand Names

Generally with high-ticket items, it is a good idea to stick to well-known brand names. At the same time, you should check out the reputation of each one. Don't just take a manufacturer's word for it. Many companies have lesser-known brands that are often cheaper, such as the dependable Roper brand made by Whirlpool. You might want to look into these as well.

The more money you spend, the more careful you should be. If a salesperson at an electronics store steers you toward a brand you never heard of, be suspicious. Odds are he or she is getting paid to push that brand.

12. Expensive Brands May Not Be As Good

You often do not get what you paid for. Consider these facts: A low priced clothes washer had the best repair record (*Consumer Reports*), a lower priced SUV did better in safety crash tests (Insurance Institute for Highway Safety), more expensive audio-visual equipment was not better than lower-priced models with the same features (*Consumer Reports*). Don't assume that paying more money means you are getting better quality. You may just be paying for a name or an image. Look for repair and reliability charts with rankings. These are worth their weight in gold.

I was considering adding a PlexWriter CD drive to my computer. I was unfamiliar with this brand so I looked for comments in the computer products newsgroups. This yielded quite a few positive remarks so I bought the device. This CD writer has worked well for years.

13. Use Newsgroups to Help You Make a Choice

With the Internet and online discussions, known as newsgroups, you can find unbiased comments about many companies and products. There is much information on customer service as well. There are literally millions of messages written by individuals that can be searched by key words. After reading a number of these, you can get a clear picture of how a product or company operates. Avoid companies where there are scores of complaints about slow service and no returned calls or e-mails. Avoid products that many have had trouble with.

14. Touching Allowed!

Many people will avoid handling merchandise on the showroom floor because they've been taught since childhood not to touch. Yet, if you are going to buy something, you need to get a feel for it. I suggest that when shopping, you open all the doors, turn knobs, set dials, press all the remote buttons, try the on-screen programming, and generally get a sense of how it works. You will be surprised how much you will learn and what this test will reveal.

Knobs on a stove should have a solid on-off click. A door on an oven that doesn't shut quite right is a sign that it is not well made. The oven temperature should be easy to set. The grates over the stove burner should sit firmly in place but move easily for cleaning. When buying furniture you should open drawers, bounce up and down on the couch, look closely at how the fabric matches and the joints are made.

15. Read the Manual in the Store

Ask to see the manual. Every device has one. With a little effort you can track it down while you are in the store. It will answer a lot of your questions much more accurately and clearly than an underpaid salesperson. Also look for a service 800 number that you can call. You might even copy important pages if you cannot make up your mind.

16. Whenever Possible, Test Drive

Today you can rent just about anything. If you are considering a computer, go to a copy center or Internet cafe and rent one for an hour. If you are exploring exercise machines, get a day pass to a health club. Try out the various devices.

Appliance Intelligence 4

How to Cook Meals and Do the Family Laundry for a Song

Overview

Don't cry too many tears when your old refrigerator finally gives up the ghost. A new fridge is much more efficient. It is likely that it will pay for itself in a few years by saving you money. The same is true for other appliances such as gas stoves and air conditioners and even clothes washers and dryers. A new energy-efficient appliance could save you 20% to 50% a year on energy costs. Major appliances are a long-term purchase lasting generally from 10 to 20 years. Take your time to make sure that you get the very best deal since you will be living with it for a long time.

Like furniture, you will need to measure the space available. I recommend a quality tape measure. Appliances not only need room, they need working room. For example, a refrigerator does not simply sit there; doors need to be opened fully so that bins and movable shelves can swing out. Side-by-side refrigerators often require less working room than top-freezer refrigera-

CAREFUL MEASURING

Ten years ago we wanted to put a clothes dryer into our older home, but had simply run out of room since we did not have a basement. Finally I realized that there was space under the stairs that had never been used. With careful measuring, I found that we would have just enough room to fit the dryer under the stairs and be able to swing open the dryer door and not hit the closet door. I had a carpenter do the work and an electrician wire the area for a 220-volt electric outlet. The fit was close but there was enough working room to haul in a basket of wet clothes.

tors with their full-sized doors. A refrigerator should be located far from any heat-producing device such as a stove or clothes dryer and should be an inch or more from the nearest wall so it can cool properly.

Always consider how you will use an appliance. You may be bringing a basket of wet clothes to your dryer. Can you get to it conveniently? Do you have enough room to open the dryer door?

With some appliances such as water heaters, dryers, and stoves, you will have to choose between gas and electric. Over the past gas has been cheaper. However, gas fumes may have to be vented.

What Buyers Need to Know

While appliances are much more standard with fewer choices than furniture or audiovisual equipment, there are still plenty of features and designs.

The price range for many appliances can go from $200 to $2000. Generally you will find the best buys, the best bang for the buck, in the mid-range. Many manufacturers use the same basic motor and configuration within certain models and then add a range of features. Even a low-priced model may give you the same essential hardware as one that is more expensive and feature laden.

Since we use appliances a lot, they naturally require some maintenance. A window air conditioner filter should be cleaned once a month in the summer and replaced periodically. When you are comparison shopping, consider how easy it is to do this important and money-saving chore. A hot water heater should be flushed out once in a while. Stoves need to be cleaned regularly. Will the top, for example, lift up with a hinged support so you can mop up any spills? You should ask to see the owners manual if you are not sure. In the showroom, do a little hands-on testing of your own to make sure that the easy-clean top is as simple as advertised.

I strongly recommend that you look for the following combination: a make and model with an excellent repair record, a popular mid-sized model, an energy-efficient design, and an appliance that is easy to service.

While this sounds complicated, it is quite simple. Repair histories are listed in the *Consumer Reports Buying Guide;* energy-use figures are posted on all new appliances in the EnergyGuide sticker, and a range of models from economy to luxury should be available on the showroom floor. See the Resources section at the end of this chapter.

Before you decide what to get, you should look at how the different choices will fit with your particular home or apartment. For example, if you decide to get a new refrigerator with

Don't Forget Maintenance

Maintenance can be a real headache and not something that many people consider when making a purchase. I bought a top-rated dishwasher only to find that I needed to change the clogged screen mesh water filter about once a year. It turned out that the filter was buried deep inside the washer and took about an hour to replace. What should have been a five-minute job was a major chore.

an ice maker, you will need to be certain it can be plumbed properly. This might mean you will have to hire a plumber to run a cold water pipe with all the right fittings behind the new fridge. A similar problem is that a new gas water heater may need to be vented.

While it is beyond the scope of this book to list every possible configuration that is now being offered, we can focus on some of the most common. You can brush up on the latest terms and offerings in a recent annual *Consumer Reports Buying Guide* listed in the Resources section at the end of this chapter.

Features That Most Experts Recommend:

- A water temperature boost on your dishwasher will save you money if you turn down the temperature on your hot water heater to 120 degrees.

- A moisture sensor that automatically shuts down a clothes dryer and runs a cool-down cycle will save you energy costs and is better for your clothes.

- Electric keypad controls cost more and may give you fewer choices than a dial setup. There is no real advantage. However, there are more problems with these and the cost of repair is high.

- A clothes washer that allows you to wash in different temperatures and different sized loads will save energy and maybe time since a small load will be done faster.

- A gas stove with an electric ignition instead of a pilot light will save about 30% on gas and also keep your kitchen cooler.

- Self-cleaning ovens work well but many experts feel that continuously cleaning models do not work as well.

- The standard refrigerator with a freezer at the top and refrigerator at the bottom is the most efficient design.

- Refrigerators with ice makers have significantly more repairs than those without.

- Side-loading clothes washers use less water and spin clothes dryer. However, these are significantly more expensive. Do the math.

How to Tweak Your Figures

When you compare models using the government's EnergyGuide sticker, realize that the energy estimate is based on a national average. Your kilowatt per hour cost may be higher or lower. You should compute this and multiply by the number of years the appliance is expected to last. This gives you the total energy cost for running that device. Write this number in a notebook along with the make and model. Refer to this figure when comparing.

- A heavy-duty motor for a clothes washer is probably worth the price unless you never try to cram too much laundry into your washer.

Learn to Recognize These Stickers

The EnergyGuide sticker is a large yellow and black sticker required by law to be on all new clothes washers, dishwashers, refrigerators, freezers, water heaters, and household heating and cooling units. Use it to compare operating costs which are based on standard U.S. Government tests. These stickers allow you to easily compute the energy costs of different makes and models because they are based on the same criteria.

Look for the distinctive voluntary Energy Star label for maximum energy savings. Products in the home appliance category covered in this book include clothes washers, dishwashers, refrigerators, and room air conditioners.

Comparison Shopping

The repair records listed in the annual *Consumer Reports Buying Guide* mentioned earlier show clearly which makes are more reliable and which ones cause problems. It appears that some more complicated devices require more repairs. Do not believe all the claims of advertising. One appliance maker that proclaims its reliability did not rank as the brand having the lowest number of repairs. And do not ignore lower cost brands: The inexpensive Roper brand had the best record of all washing machines in the *1998 Consumer Reports Buying Guide*, a much better record than others that were more expensive.

I Found Newer Was More Efficient

The electric ignition in our new gas stove uses a lot less gas and keeps the kitchen cooler in the hot North Carolina summers. It is much better than the old pilot light system. Even the new washing machine does a better job of spinning clothes so that the dryer does not have to work as hard to dry them.

Naturally you will need to decide exactly which features you really do need and which you can live without before you walk into a store to do some serious buying. If you don't, you will be dazzled by an array of choices that can confuse you. Most people can be talked into spending more than they planned. With so many features it's hard to know where to stop. At the web site of a major discount warehouse store, I counted 321 refrigerators from $267 to $1956.

I would also suggest that you do some research into very energy-efficient designs. One new refrigerator uses only as much electricity as a lightbulb. I have already mentioned the U.S. Government's Energy Star program; you can browse some of the latest energy efficient designs at their site: www.energystar.gov.

Before Shopping

In addition to carefully measuring the space for the new appliance, you should measure all the doors, stairs, elevators, and hallways that must be negotiated to deliver it. This is your responsibility. If you order a stove and it is delivered as promised, but it is too large to be moved into your apartment, it is your fault. According to one major appliance retailer, "Unfortunately, not fitting into the space intended is the main reason appliances get returned." You should also double-check that the appropriate electric outlet for the device will be within reach of the electric cord, usually within a distance of 3.5 feet.

Just how large a refrigerator or air conditioner do you need? A half full fridge does not run efficiently. You want a refrigerator that will be roomy but not empty and an AC that will run the cooling compressor 80% of the time. The same goes for freezer compartments and also stand-alone freezers. A large water heater which keeps water hot all the time, may be quite costly if you don't use that much hot water.

Also decide just how much you want to pay for appearance. If you buy a nonstandard color, you may pay extra and it may have to be special ordered. If you would like all your appliances in the same nonstandard color, you may be forced to buy from the same manufacturer to get the color to match exactly. It is unlikely that you will find a precise color match, other than white, from two different manufacturers. So to get your color scheme just right you might get a great stove but be forced to buy a dishwasher with a poor repair record.

Buyer Beware

Major appliance stores may offer a good deal but then tack on expensive delivery and setup charges. Some do not set up at all, but rather leave you to hire a workman to finish the job. I prefer the local appliance store because the price is usually more competitive when all is added in. Plus you'll get brownie points for being a loyal customer, which comes in handy if you have any

Installation Costs

A friend of ours replaced her hot water heater. While the unit was not that expensive, only about $150, the plumbing cost was estimated at $300. She shopped around and found another store that would do that plumbing for $100 less.

problems down the road. My local store carries the same brands as the large chain megastore, but has a better understanding of local needs and conditions. The store would not sell a window air conditioner with aluminum cooling tubes because on the coast the salt water would quickly corrode these air conditioners, shortening their life considerably.

Beware of new and untried technologies. In the near future, there will be microwave clothes dryers, which should dry clothes faster and more efficiently. However, don't be the first on your block to own one—let other people be the guinea pigs. With a new system, it will take some years to work out all the bugs and then the price usually drops. Buy that microwave dryer five or so years after it first comes out.

Discount Strategies

Best Single Strategy
Buy An Appliance During a Regular Sale

New appliances are better and more efficient. I recommend shopping for them new when they are on sale, then haggle for a better discount and perhaps free delivery and setup.

Major appliances on sale: January, July, October, and November.

Specific appliances:

Air conditioners: February and July.

Laundry appliances: March.

1. Comparison shopping

By following the steps in the Comparison Shopping section in this chapter, you should be able to locate the lowest retail price for the most reliable and well-designed model with only those features that you really need.

2. Haggling for a low price

In the appliance business, bargaining is standard. Always try for a lower price. Simply ask, "What is the best price you can give me for this refrigerator?"

3. Haggling for extras

Ask for free delivery, free installation and setup, and/or free disposal of your old appliance.

4. Custom configurations

Does not apply.

5. Regular sales

This is the best single strategy for getting a great deal. Please read about this in more detail at the top of this Discount Strategies section.

6. Rebates

You should ask the store about manufacturer's rebates and check the manufacturer's web site. In the past there have been rebates during the off months especially for dishwashers and refrigerators.

7. Unusual discounts and sales

In a slow economy you may find special financing, special sales, and salespeople who are much more willing to deal.

8. Internet shopping and mail order

You can buy appliances from a large warehouse and have them shipped. I do not recommend buying this way since returning a defective one could be a major problem. However, a major chain home improvement warehouse, such as Lowe's (www.lowes.com), allows you to browse and compare appliances, order online, and then have the appliance delivered by the local store to your home. The web site even checks the inventory at your local store. Sears (www.sears.com) also offers a similar service on their web site. Comparison of different prices and features is much easier this way.

9. Outlet stores and outlet malls

If you find an appliance outlet close to you, it might be a good deal.

10. Closeouts and discontinued models

When the newer models are coming in and the older ones are still on the floor, you can save a bundle by taking these off the dealer's hands. You might even check the manufacturer's web site to find which models were discontinued recently.

11. Floor models, demonstrators, scratch-and-dent, blemished seconds

It is not unusual for a dealer to have a clothes washer with a minor ding that might not even be noticed. However, this cosmetic blemish will save you a ton of money. Bargain for the lowest price on a flawless model and then ask for another 10% to 20% off on one with a minor surface flaw.

12. Refurbished

You will probably not find many refurbished appliances.

13. Used

For a variety of reasons I do not recommend buying appliances used. New appliances tend to be more efficient. A used one will, in the long run, cost you more.

14. Financing

Some appliance stores advertise deals such as 90 days same as cash. Take advantage of this if you can pay for it in 90 days instead of putting it on a credit card. Read the fine print! In many agreements, if you miss the 90-day deadline for final payment, you will find that interest on your purchase will go back to the day you bought it. The store interest rate can be 20% or higher. The 90-day period should start when your appliance is delivered to your home and not when you close the deal, since it could be weeks before it arrives. Ask for a discount if you pay cash.

15. Extra discounts

If you buy two appliances at the same time ask for a volume discount. During a regular sales month you might buy two appliances, one of which is a floor model and the other a scratch-and-dent. In addition to the sale discount, you should get an extra savings when you buy the floor model and also the scratch-and-dent. Because you are buying two, ask for a volume discount or free delivery and setup.

Making the Deal

Before you decide on a price ask about delivery costs, setup costs, and disposal costs of your old appliance. If the dealer won't budge on the cost of the appliance, ask for free delivery or setup. Once you have agreed, get an official invoice form, which lists the make, model, and color of the appliance, the price for the appliance, the agreed cost of delivery, setup, additional installation, disposal if necessary, and sales tax. The expected delivery date should be stated clearly. People often forget about requiring a firm date for delivery and then wait for weeks. If you have made any other arrangements such as payment in 90 days with no interest, make sure that this is spelled out on the invoice. Take a copy of the complete financial agreement if the full details are on a separate sheet.

After the Sale

Do not remove your old appliance until the new one arrives, or you may end up eating out of a cooler for a week or cooking on a hot plate. After your new appliance is delivered, have your old one removed.

As with any device you should check all the various features immediately to make sure that they work properly. You should write down any problems as they occur and immediately notify the vendor, as the store may want to refer you to a repair service instead of replacing the appliance or refunding the purchase price.

Many appliances come with a sticker on the side stating the specifications of the device. Save this sticker by removing it from the appliance and then adhering to a piece of paper that you file with the guarantee.

Resources

BOOKS

You should be able to find the following books at www.Amazon.com.

For detailed repair histories of major appliances and reviews of new appliances buy the most recent edition of:

Consumer Reports Buying Guide, $9.99, Consumer Reports.

Smart Questions for Savvy Shoppers, The Guide That Gets You the Most for Your Dollar, by Dorothy Leeds with Sharyn Kolberg, $8.99, HarperPaperbacks, 1994.

INTERNET

I have created an updated and comprehensive list of useful appliance web sites at the web page for this book at:

www.savvydiscounts.com/thebook

You can go to the U.S. Government's Energy Star site and browse some of the latest energy-efficient designs at:

www.energystar.gov

These are the web addresses of well-known appliance brands:

www.frigidaire.com

www.hotpoint.com

www.kitchenaid.com

www.maytag.com

www.whirlpool.com

If you live near a Lowe's Home Improvement Warehouse you can browse appliances online and check inventory at your local store. Sears offers the same service:

www.lowes.com

www.sears.com

The following site sells appliances on the Internet and ships directly to the consumer:

www.appliancediscountwarehouse.com

For feedback about appliances:

www.epinions.com

Search the archives of newsgroups for letters relating to service or product reliability:

groups.google.com

You can also post questions on the appropriate newsgroup.
To check if there have been any unresolved complaints with a dealer go to the Better Business Bureau site:

www.bbb.com

Audiovisual Delights 5

Channel-Surf with Your Big-Screen TV, but Will it Work with HDTV?

Overview

Unfortunately, the retail electronics business has its share of bad practices. Some tactics are even illegal. This is enough to make a buyer quite wary from the outset. In addition the technology is confusing and keeps changing, TV is moving toward High Definition TV (HDTV), there are a bunch of different formats for recording with a camcorder, and do you really need all the AUX and plug-in openings on a boom box ?

I recommend that you tackle one product at a time and become familiar with it before you walk into a store. You should compare prices at three different places at least. One of those places might be the Internet. Since audiovisual equipment is quite technical you can go to a manufacturer's product page to read an overview. You can also print out the specifications (spec sheet). This page is very valuable because it allows you to compare features. Read more about specifications and spec sheets in the Introduction.

What Buyers Need to Know

With formats and technology changing so quickly, it is beyond the scope of this book to list every possible feature and configuration that is now being offered. You can brush up on the latest features and terms used to describe them in a recent annual *Consumer Reports Buying Guide* listed in the Resources section at the end of this chapter.

Terms

While you may be familiar with many of these terms, with the onset of digital technology, it is important to understand some of the new capabilities. Digital technology is coming on strong but costs significantly more in most cases. Expect the cost of digital to drop as it becomes more common.

> **Camcorder:** the general term for a camera that records moving pictures. It records on a tape compatible with either a VCR or a DVD.
>
> **CD:** Compact Disk. It looks exactly like a DVD disk but holds much less information.
>
> **Combination DVD/VCR:** just like vinyl records, videotapes are going to be around for a long time. This has led to a proliferation of combination DVD players and VCRs. And while DVDs may look great, recording on this format is still quite

expensive. With this device you can use the VCR to record off the TV. At the moment this might be the best of both worlds.

Digital Camera: a still camera that takes pictures compatible with computers. These images can be put on the Internet, sent as e-mail, placed on a CD, printed out, or even shown on a TV.

Digital TV: a television that accepts digital pictures. DVDs will look much sharper on a digital TV.

DV: Digital Video, video recorded in a digital format. This has better quality and is much easier to edit than older videotape. These images can be transferred and reworked in a computer.

DVD: Digital Video Disk. It can store complete movies on 5" disks. It looks like the older CD but holds a lot more information.

Flat Screen: a digital screen that is only several inches deep.

High Definition TV (HDTV): This new television standard has been mandated by the U.S. Government. It will show a wider and much sharper picture.

Home Theater: a large screen that displays a TV or DVD image. It often includes Surround Sound.

Patching and Patch Cords: When you connect two devices with a cable you are patching. Understanding how to do this is crucial with a component system. If you want to run the sound from your cable TV converter into an amplifier instead of your TV, you will need to understand this as well. I recommend lots of in and out plug-in openings because these are relatively cheap and give you more flexibility to patch any way you want.

71

> ## We Can Look Forward to 5 Years of TV Hell
>
> **With the change from analog to digital TV and from the standard TV format to the high definition format (HDTV), you can expect lots of problems. "We are about to go through five years of TV hell," said Josh Bernoff with Forrester Research quoted in *USA Today* in 2002. Be wary of claims of future compatibility. Don't buy new expensive technology until you must. The price of digital TV should start to fall sharply as more sets are made.**

Surround Sound: a four channel format that uses typically five speakers to surround the listener with sound. In combination with DVD and a home theater, it creates a high quality audiovisual experience.

VCR: Video Cassette Recorder.

Look for This Label

Look for the distinctive Energy Star label for maximum energy savings. Products in the audiovisual category include televisions, VCRs, combination units, DVD products, home audio, and set-top boxes.

The Audiovisual Jungle

Many salespeople at electronic stores are paid by commission. They often get hefty bonuses for pushing certain products and

Audiovisual Mumbo Jumbo

I have a very simple rule of thumb when it comes to technical salespeople. When they start using lots of big words, they probably don't know what they are talking about and it is time to walk out the door. People should be able to explain a feature in plain English, then demonstrate that feature for you. If they cannot make the feature work on the sales floor, don't assume that it will work okay at home.

they probably don't know much more about electronics than you do. What this means is that you should not ask salespeople for advice about which model to choose. It is almost certain that they will recommend the more expensive one or the one that gives them the best commission that week. You might ask a salesperson to explain features that are available plus the advantages and disadvantages.

There is a lot of jargon associated with stereos, TVs, camcorders, VCRs, digital cameras, and DVD players. To the uninitiated, this can be very intimidating. To add to the confusion, some terms apply to all brands and some are flashy names created by manufacturers just for their own products. Many features sound good but are not all that useful. For example, picture-in-picture which allows you to watch one channel in a small area while viewing another channel seems to be a great idea. However, a survey found that people simply did not use it unless they were ardent sports fans and wanted to follow several games at once.

Don't Get Oversold

A new novel by Ben Cheever really gets to the heart of what selling is all about in the electronics industry today. When he was selling computers and electronics he was taught that, "A clerk sells a customer what he or she had intended to buy for what he or she had intended to pay. A salesman, on the other hand, sells the customer more than he or she meant to buy, for more than he or she had expected to pay. A home run . . . meant not only the sale of the highest-priced product possible, but also the accessories, the insurance, and the store credit card." *Selling Ben Cheever: Back to Square One in a Service Economy* by Ben Cheever, Bloomsbury, 286 pages, $25.95.

Before Shopping

Do your research, compare spec sheets, but remember exactly what your needs are. You don't want to get overwhelmed by the possibilities. Most audiovisual purchases will last about five to ten years, so you should plan with the future in mind, but don't buy features you don't need.

Preparation will make you much less likely to succumb to the siren song of the salesperson at the electronics store who has this great deal on a camcorder with all these features you never heard of made by a company whose name you don't recognize.

If you are buying large equipment such as a home theater, you should also consider where it will fit in your house or apartment. The larger the equipment, the more measuring and planning will be required.

Comparison Shopping

As with other products in this book, you will find a wide range of prices and features from a color TV that sells for less than $100 to a large home theater TV screen that sells for about $3,000. In between those prices you will be offered a myriad of choices and you will have to decide exactly what features you really need.

I recommend that you look at the repair graphs in the annual *Consumer Reports Buying Guide* (see the Resources section at the end of this chapter for details). The repair records are unbiased and can reveal some surprising facts. They are not an opinion but rather a simple graphing of repair reports from ten of thousands of people who have had experiences with various brand names. To my surprise I found that a low priced Emerson VCR had about half as many repairs as a well respected top of the line model.

Comparison pricing is critical with electronics. Prices can vary widely. You would not know this if you walked into one store and simply bought something off the shelf. The best way to comparison shop is to read inserts and fliers in the Sunday newspaper from department, electronics, or office stores. You should also compare prices on the Internet.

You will find good detailed reviews of many of these audiovisual devices in *Consumer Reports*. However, do not blindly

Get the Biggest Bang for Your Buck

Look for good deals in the mid-price range. For example, a midsized TV in the 25–27 inch range will often have the best quality and features for the lowest price.

follow the reviews you read there. While their reviews are excellent and their rating system is helpful, it is only one opinion. Unless the model you are considering is rated unacceptable, you should follow your instincts and buy what seems like the best deal for your needs.

BUYER BEWARE

The phrase "buyer beware" applies to the electronics industry more than most. Here are some of the things to watch for:

1. Selling refurbished merchandise as new

One survey of these stores found that half were selling remanufactured merchandise as new. This is illegal, but it can be very hard to tell. Make sure that you receive a sealed box that has come straight from the manufacturer and check that the serial number on the box matches the item you bought. There is nothing wrong with buying a refurbished item as long as you know what it is and have received an appropriate discount.

2. Selling products at a low price while leaving out accessories that were part of the original manufacturer's package, sometimes known as stock splitting

Some dealers will advertise a low price which they will honor but then charge you for accessories that should have been included in the original box.

3. Gray market items

The "gray market" refers to items that were intended for sale outside the U.S. but were imported into this country. While this practice is legal, they do not usually come with a U.S. guarantee. You may have to send the equipment overseas to get it repaired! Typically U.S. rebates are not honored for gray market products either.

4. Extended warranties

Salespeople will push and push these as good deals but they are not. These are simply a bad use of your money. Please read more about these in the Introduction.

5. Store credit

If you came into the store with a dollar amount in mind and now are considering store credit to buy a more expensive model, there is probably something wrong. Store credit is often very expensive. There is usually no need for you to pay more than you planned, if you have done your homework.

6. Restocking fees

While you are probably used to returning a piece of clothing you did not like and getting a full refund, electronics and audiovisual products are different. Restocking fees are common in mail order, for example, but now even retail stores are beginning to add this charge. In 2002 Target Stores started charging a restocking fee for electronics. Businesses that charge this fee will let you exchange a defective device for a new one at no charge. However, if you return an item simply because you do not like it, you can be charged a 10% to 20% restocking fee.

7. Accessories

Try out your new VCR before you decide that you want that separate rewinder. Salespeople have a way of tacking on all kinds of accessories that you never knew you needed. Remember you can always go back to the store. There are very simple ways to avoid all of these problems:

1. Buy from an authorized dealer. An authorized dealer is one who has been approved by the manufacturer. You may find that some stores are authorized dealers for some companies and other stores for other companies.

2. Do not buy any gray market items. You will only save a small amount of money. If the product has to be repaired, it will be costly and time-consuming.

3. Stay within your budget and forget about store credit, extended warranties, and accessories you can buy later.

4. Avoid retail stores with restocking fees. Don't order audiovisual stuff through the web or via mail order, unless you know exactly what you want.

Discount Strategies

The Best Single Strategy
Buy Discontinued or Closeout Audiovisual Equipment

That shiny new stereo is tomorrow's closeout. Electronic goods are a gold mine for these kinds of discounts. Models change frequently and all models are discontinued eventually. You can save a bundle by staying just a little behind the times. You might even look first at these before considering anything else. Make sure you get a full warranty. Prime months for finding these are January through March.

Check web sites for closeouts and discounts. For example, Sears has a regular clearance center. See a list of web addresses at the end of this chapter.

1. Comparison shopping

By following the steps in the Comparison Shopping section in this chapter, you should be able to locate the lowest retail price for the most reliable and well-designed brand-name merchandise with only those features that you really need.

2. Haggling for a low price

The more you pay, the more you can haggle. While haggling is not as common in audiovisual equipment as other products, you should be able to deal when buying expensive items.

3. Haggling for extras

Ask the salesperson to throw in some videotapes with a VCR, or batteries with a digital camera.

4. Custom configurations

You can design your own stereo system by purchasing components rather than buying an all-in-one model. If you know how to patch components together, you can get a better system at a lower cost.

5. Regular sales

Audiovisual equipment: February and July. TVs: May.

6. Rebates

You may be able to find rebates, especially for more expensive equipment such as digital cameras, camcorders, and home theaters. Some stores now post rebates in special sections of their store. You can also check the manufacturers' web sites.

7. Unusual discounts and sales

When the economy is bad, you may notice a number of special deals that are not normally available. Some stores offer 0% financing in hard economic times, and some manufacturers or stores will put you on their special offer e-mail list. Internet and mail order companies have regular offers of free shipping during slow periods.

8. Internet shopping and mail order

If you are certain about the exact make and model you want, you can save a substantial amount of money getting a product shipped to you. See our checklist about ordering in the chapter about the Internet and mail order. Some large well-known stores such as Circuit City, Best Buy, and Sears now have extensive web sites where you can browse without all the noise and confusion. Office supply stores carry a number of these items as well. See the Resources section at the end of this chapter for web addresses.

9. Outlet stores and outlet malls

You should be able to find a wealth of makes and models at outlets. If you live far from these stores, make sure that you can return a defective product through the mail. Check that you will be receiving a full warranty.

You can get a directory of about 14,000 outlets in the USA and Canada from www.outletbound.com. You can search by location, store, brand, or category.

There are also quite a few online factory outlets. You may find a variety of discounted new products. Large manufacturers often have their own online factory outlets. Check their web sites.

10. Closeouts and discontinued models

This is the best single strategy for getting a great deal. Please read about this in more detail at the top of the Discount Strategies section.

11. Floor models, demonstrators, scratch-and-dent, blemished, seconds

When you walk into a large electronics store that sells audiovisual equipment, you will see dozens of TVs, camcorders, boom boxes, and digital cameras on display for the consumer to handle. Sooner or later all of these will be sold as floor models or demonstrators. When the models change, you should ask about the price of a floor model. New TVs, for example, are often introduced in the fall.

12. Refurbished

You will find a wealth of refurbished equipment. These often sell for 30% off or more. Make sure you get a full warranty. Refurbished can be an excellent buy.

If you do a search of the Internet, you can find a number of businesses that sell refurbished audiovisual products. See the guidelines for dealing with these companies in the chapter on the Internet and mail order.

13. Used

Buying used audiovisual equipment is usually not a good idea. Generally these do not sell at a significant discount. Why buy an old TV for $75 that may break in five years and does not have the latest features. Instead you can buy a new TV with stereo sound and a crisp picture for $200 plus a warranty. While I recommend buying used for a number of items listed in this book, I would try to get audiovisual equipment new.

14. Financing

Avoid store credit, which can be over 20%. A low-interest credit card might be the best way to go, if you make a regular payment each month for the same amount. If you are offered a no-interest or no-payments deal for six to twelve months, ask for a discount if you pay cash.

15. Extra discounts

If you buy several items together, such as a TV and a DVD player, ask for a volume discount.

Example of combined discounts:

Here is an example of a combined discount: A discontinued (1st discount) floor model (2nd discount) at the end of the season (3rd discount) should sell at a substantial savings since you are getting three discounts rolled into one product.

Making the Deal

No matter where you buy you should ask these questions before signing on the dotted line:

Will I get a brand-new item in the original box as shipped by the manufacturer?

Is it gray market?

Don't Be in a Hurry to Buy New Technology

The price of technology keeps dropping. The first reasonably priced VCR was a low $1,000 in 1977; ten years later VCRs were selling for $300. You can expect this same pattern with digital TV, HDTV, digital tuners, and DVD recorders.

Does it have a full United States warranty?

What is your refund policy? If there is a problem, how many days do I have before I must return it to the store for a refund or exchange? Do you charge a restocking fee? If so how much is the restocking fee?

How long is the warranty for this product?

After the Sale

Immediately after you take possession, you should check the box. Because there have been so many shenanigans with the electronics retail sector, many manufacturers and reputable stores only deliver the goods in sealed boxes as shipped by the manufacturer. Follow this checklist:

First: Was the box sealed? If the item was new, it should be in a sealed box from the manufacturer. Also check that the model serial number on the outside of the box matches the serial number on the product on the inside.

Second: Is everything in the box that should be there? You should find a list either on the outside or on a separate sheet inside the box that states all that is included. With an item such as a digital camera, there can be quite a number of essential accessories such as the battery, the battery charger, patch cords that go into the back of a TV, and cords that connect to a computer.

Third: Is there a warranty card that specifies the length of the warranty and that is good in the U.S.?

If any of the above is out of order, you should return the box with all its parts immediately to the store and demand a refund or a new factory sealed box.

As we pointed out in the Introduction of this book, you should *not* fill out the warranty card until you can no longer return it to the store. Once you fill out the warranty card you are not dealing with the store and getting a refund or exchange; instead you are dealing with the manufacturer and getting an item repaired.

Turn the device on and leave it on for at least 24 hours. This is called a burn-in and most problems with electronics will show up at this early stage. If the device has a lot of features, try them out. Be sure to read the manual thoroughly. With a camcorder you should zoom in and out, record sound, pan the camera into

Reading the Manual

I had learned only one method for transferring my pictures files from my Sony CD1000 camera to the computer, which was via the computer's CD drive. After a year the computer drive was taking a very long time to read the CD created in the camera. So I went back, reread the manual, and switched to option B which was to connect the camera via USB, and it worked much better.

very bright and very dark areas. Then you should play the tape back. You should keep all those original boxes. If you ever need to return the gizmo for a repair, some manufacturers require them.

Resources

BOOKS
You should be able to find the following books at www.Amazon.com.

For detailed repair histories of audiovisual equipment and reviews of new products buy the most recent edition of:

Consumer Reports Buying Guide, $9.99, Consumer Reports.

Smart Questions for Savvy Shoppers: The Guide That Gets You the Most for Your Dollar, by Dorothy Leeds with Sharyn Kolberg, $8.99, HarperPaperbacks, 1994.

INTERNET
I have created an updated and comprehensive list of useful audiovisual web sites at the web page for this book at:

www.savvydiscounts.com/thebook

You can go to the U.S. Government's Energy Star site and browse some of the latest energy efficient designs at:

www.energystar.gov

Addresses of major manufacturers:

www.hitachi.com   *www.sony.com*

www.jvc.com   *www.sylvania.com*

www.kenwood.com   *www.teac.com*

www.magnavox.com   *www.toshiba.com*

www.panasonic.com   *www.yamaha.com*

www.rca.com   *www.zenith.com*

www.sanyo.com

Two major retailers:

www.bhphotovideo.com

www.radioshack.com

J&R Music has been in business for 31 years and enjoys a good reputation. Browse the site for audio or video equipment and cameras. You can even check out a list of closeouts:

www.jandr.com

Try these office supply stores with catalogues and excellent web sites. Some list clearance technology, have a general clearance center and an online rebate center. Most carry digital cameras and other audiovisual equipment:

www.officedepot.com

www.officemax.com

www.quillcorp.com

www.staples.com

www.viking.com

To comparison shop on the Web for audiovisual products:

shopping.yahoo.com

www.BizRate.com

www.Cnet.com

www.Dealtime.com

www.PriceGrabber.com

For reviews and opinions:

www.epinions.com

www.reviewboard.com

Search the archives of newsgroups for letters relating to service or product reliability:

groups.google.com

You can also post questions on the appropriate newsgroup.

To check if there have been any unresolved complaints with a dealer go to the Better Business Bureau site:

www.bbb.com

Automobile Attractions 6

Don't Get Taken for a Ride

Overview

The ideal car purchase would be a great deal on a comfortable automobile that required low insurance premiums and low maintenance, was reliable and needed few repairs, was considered safe in a crash, got great gas mileage, and that held its resale value. Is there such a vehicle? The answer is a resounding yes in just about any category you want to pick: economy, minivan, SUV, and luxury car. The trick is to go through the various ratings and find the ones that meet all these criteria.

Crunching these numbers used to be quite difficult and time-consuming. Now with the help of the Internet, the job is easy. I will go into more detail about Web resources later in this chapter.

Buying a car is usually three transactions not just one. It is easy to get a good deal at one end and get taken at the other. The smart consumer will separate these as much as possible so that they don't get mingled together and disguise the true costs. Negotiate each one by itself.

The three transactions are these:

1. Buying the car, whether it is new or used

2. Financing the purchase

3. Selling or trading in your old vehicle

For example, some dealerships will give you a great bargain on the new car and then a lowball figure for your trade-in.

As with everything in this book, it helps to do your homework. You should walk into a showroom with a clear idea of how much you should pay for a new make and model with accessories. In addition, before making a deal, you should have compared interest rates at your bank, on the Internet, and at other dealerships. You should be aware of any financing specials that are being offered by dealers. Last, you should know how much your old car would fetch as a trade-in and on the open market. You can save or make a considerable amount of money by selling the car yourself. In one calculation I made, based on information on the Web, a person could trade in a 1998 car in 2002 for $5,175 or sell it personally for $7,030, a difference of $1,855 or over 30% more than the trade-in amount.

What Buyers Need to Know

There are a number of terms specific to car sales that are useful to know because they will help you in your negotiations.

MSRP: Manufacturers Suggested Retail Price.

Dealer holdback or pack: a percent that many dealers will be credited by the manufacturer from the sale of a car. Typically it is 2% to 3% of the MSRP but this practice does not include all manufacturers. Factor in this amount when negotiating for a fair price. Edmunds.com lists the holdback percentages for most manufacturers.

Carryover: a term used for last year's new car that is still sitting in the dealer's lot after the new models have been introduced (NMI). Once a car becomes a carryover, a dealer may receive a 5% rebate from the manufacturer which could be passed on to the buyer.

NMI: new model introduction or when the new models have been officially introduced.

Monroney sticker: This white sticker on the car's window is mandated by federal law. It must show the MSRP base price, the options installed at the factory, freight charges, and estimated mpg. No one can remove this sticker except the buyer.

Dealer invoice: the price that the dealer was billed by the manufacturer for the car and factory-installed options. This cost does not include dealer holdbacks (see above), rebates, incentives, or bonuses to the dealer.

While most people are familiar with basic car terms, some new words and concepts are entering the world of automobiles, such as:

Telematics: Still in the development stages, telematics is the combination of computers and wireless telecommunications. At the moment applications for cars such as satellite radio and

Global Positioning System navigation are available. This capability is expected to grow rapidly in the near future.

GPS: The satellite Global Positioning System will be used increasingly for automobile navigation.

Before Shopping

Before you go onto a car lot to make a serious negotiation you need to know whether you want to buy a new car, lease a new car, buy a late-model car, or buy an older car. Let's take these one by one:

BUYING A NEW CAR

The longer you drive a new car, the more value you will receive. You will know exactly what repairs have been done and how the car has been maintained. If you are the kind of person who likes to trade for a new car every couple of years, you will be paying more overall because most depreciation occurs in the first few years of ownership. However, you will probably spend less time getting your car serviced and repaired as these chores and their associated costs increase significantly as the car gets older. The choice is up to you.

LEASING A NEW CAR

For a few people leasing might be a good deal. Businesses and organizations might prefer leasing since in many cases there is a tax benefit. Yet for the rest of us, leasing stinks. Lease contracts are hard to understand and hard to read; there are odd terms, penalties, and charges specific only to leasing. You cannot really compare interest rates because you are not borrowing, you are paying for the use of the car over time. The three transactions of getting the new car, trading in the old car, and finding a low interest rate are all jumbled together in a way that few people can calculate. In addition, there are a number of leasing companies and agreements, not just those offered by the major car makers. These second tier leases may be especially confusing and full of surprises. The bottom line is this: When you buy a car and the loan is paid off, you own the car; when you get a lease and the lease is up, you own nothing.

BUYING A LATE-MODEL USED CAR

If you buy a late-model used car, you can get top quality, a substantial discount, plus current and tested technology. Never buy a used car without looking at the repair history for that particular model. Always pay to have a mechanic thoroughly check all systems. Never buy such a car without checking its history through a service like CarFax.com and verifying, among other things, that the mileage on the odometer is accurate and that the car has not been in an accident. This same advice holds true for buying an older model used car in the next section.

You can buy a late-model car from a new car dealer, a used car lot, or an individual. I would recommend buying from either a new car dealership where regulations are a bit stricter than used car lots or buying from an individual.

BUYING AN OLDER MODEL USED CAR

If you decide to buy an older model, the repair history for the model is even more important. Defects are bound to show up as the car ages. Yet it is quite possible to buy a car with 80,000 miles on it and run it for years of satisfactory and reliable operation.

With an older model I recommend buying from an individual. After years of buying cars in this market myself, I have found that dealers do not know the background of the used cars they sell. They have often bought the car from a wholesaler and don't have the time or money to have it checked out. While they might vacuum the inside and polish the outside, the parts that really count such as the engine are pretty much ignored. As long as the car starts okay and doesn't send a cloud of smoke out the back,

Rick's Incredibly Simple Used Car Test

Before you go to the bother and expense to have a used car checked out by a mechanic, you can run this simple test that will give you an excellent idea of how a used car is running. You don't need tools or have to open the hood! I recommend doing this on a highway when there is little or no traffic. Drive a car, that has warmed-up for at least five minutes, from a full stop to about 55 MPH, accelerating smoothly and quickly. Notice how the gears shift, any hesitation, any roughness in the running of the engine, any shaking of the tires, body, or steering wheel. Take your hands off the steering wheel for just a moment. Does the car drift to one side or the other? Then bring the vehicle to a full stop. As you apply the brakes, does it pull left or right when you take your hands briefly off the wheel? If possible, swerve the car to the left then to the right; does it sway too much? If it passes all these tests, the auto is probably running fine; if not, run the test again and note any problems. If it passes this test and you like the car, take it to a mechanic for a more thorough look. If you are unsure, report the results to a mechanic. He or she may be able to diagnose any trouble.

the dealer is satisfied. Individuals will generally sell a car for a lot less than a new car dealership, perhaps halfway between the trade-in value for the car and the retail value as listed by a used car Blue Book service.

Make sure that the individual is really an individual and not a used car dealer who is trying to appear like a good old Joe. You can usually determine this quite quickly by asking a few personal questions such as, "How long have you owned it? What work have you done on it?"

If you buy from an individual you can often get a list of the repairs that this person has made. Many people are surprisingly candid about problems and defects, much more so than dealers. The ideal purchase, of course, is a five-to-ten-year-old car, owned by only one person who kept all the receipts for repairs. Such a deal is not that hard to locate. If you are calling around about used cars from ads you find in the auto classifieds, you should ask the sellers whether they have such receipts and how long they personally have owned the car.

If you would prefer to buy from a dealer, you might try a service such as CarMax® that runs all used cars through a "certified quality inspection," allows a five-day money-back guarantee on any car you buy, a limited 30-day warranty, and a clean title guarantee. The only drawback is that you cannot haggle over the price, but then CarMax also claims to show its cars in a low-pressure environment. While this service is only in a limited number of states at the moment, you should expect more businesses like this to start popping up all over the country, since they take the hassle (and haggle) out of used car buying.

Some well-known car manufacturers have their own used car quality-control programs such as the Honda Certified Used Vehicles which according to Honda, "are inspected, certified, and backed to factory-created standards from Honda." Call local dealers and ask them about the quality of their used cars.

RECOMMENDATION

I believe that the very best deal is often a late-model used car. There are a variety of reasons for this, some not so obvious.

First: Most depreciation occurs in the first couple of years. You may be able to get a low mileage four-year-old car for as much as 50% off the new price.

Second: When you buy a car, you don't just pay the negotiated price. You pay sales tax, insurance, and often county taxes. The lower the initial price of the car, the lower these other associated costs will be.

Third: A used car has a model specific repair history. A new car does not. It's that simple. After two years it is easy to discover which models had problems and which ones were reliable. Even a popular car that has not gone through a major model change can have hidden problems. The *Consumer Reports Annual Buying Guide* lists detailed auto reliability reports on sixteen different vehicle components. These reports cover models going back eight years and are compiled from as many as

How My Father Taught Me

My father never bought a car new. Instead he would buy a two-year-old model. As a child, I wondered why he did this. When our neighbors bought a new 1957 Chevy, I asked my dad why we drove an old 1955 Ford. "You pay too much for a new car," was about all he said. Now as an adult, I understand.

600,000 vehicles. See the Resources section at the end of this chapter for more details.

If you pick a two-to-four-year-old model that has a better than average reliability, you are getting a great deal. Not only are you paying a lot less than for a new car, you are getting one with a proven track record.

Of course there are great deals in the new car market and with offers such as zero percent financing, you may find them hard to resist. Nevertheless it is smart to avoid models that have gone through a major retooling.

Comparison Shopping

Before getting too serious, you might window-shop using the Internet or look at a number of publications that should be available at your local newsstand. On the Internet you will find a wealth of information. Some you may have to pay for, but in many cases you will not. For example, Edmunds.com, allows you to calculate the full cost of buying a new vehicle including depreciation, mileage, repairs, and insurance over a five-year period. Other calculations such as whether to trade in a car or sell it yourself are available. There are also simple methods for determining a fair price for a used car. See the Resources section at the end of this chapter for more details.

In addition, there are a number of newsstand publications that are excellent. For example, the comprehensive *Consumer-Guide Car and Truck Test Buying Guide* lists latest dealer invoice and retail prices for just about every new car available. It includes a listing of comparable cars in each category and rates all cars in the publication. Never trust only one review; read several including one in a car magazine.

Small Cars Are Safe Today

Don't be afraid of small cars when it comes to safety. Newer small cars have done exceptionally well in tests conducted by the Insurance Institute for Highway Safety. To see about specific results, go to their web site: www.hwysafety.org

For used cars you might check local "trader" publications that list sales of used cars by individuals and dealers. These local guides can give you a good feel for the prices in your area which can vary widely from region to region. You can also get a copy of the comprehensive *Used Car Prices* by Vehicle Market Research International. Make sure that you get the most current issue for each publication.

Since you may have your car for a number of years, I recommend that you buy a fairly standard popular model. If you drive it for a while, you will find that down the road you will have less trouble locating parts and mechanics who know how to repair it.

To really compare car costs you need to know the following:

1. The price for several different cars. Start with the MSRP or dealer invoice. I'll talk about discounting this price later.

2. The options you want: which are standard, what are extra, which ones you want that come in a package deal, what extras you don't want that also come in the package deal, what extras you can add on later yourself—these are known as aftermarket products.

3. How well your selected cars stack up in crash tests both for the cost of repairs and possible injury to yourself or your passengers.

4. Cost of insurance for the various cars.

5. Gas mileage and cost per year for gas and maintenance.

6. Cost of repairs for each choice based on the history of the model. Assume you will pay more for repairs as the years progress.

7. Resale value of your various choices after three to five years based on past resale values for the same make and model.

8. Interest rates: Determine the cost of company financing if you choose to get a loan through the car dealer; comparison shop for loans on the Internet; call your bank or credit union. You will pay more for a loan for a used car than a new car.

9. Rebates and incentives if available. Some of these may be available to you the customer, but others are only available to the dealer. It is then up to the dealership whether to pass its savings on to you. You will need to do some research so that you know about current offers.

10. Cost and time involved if you get a special order and have the car made for you in the factory.

11. Reputable dealers who sell these cars. Remember after the sale you will be coming back to the dealer, not the manufacturer, for problems and regular maintenance. Check the Better Business Bureau for any complaints or

ask someone who has bought from the dealer. Since dealers often put stickers on the rear of new cars they sell, you might ask an owner with such a sticker about the dealership. The reputation of the service department may be even more important, since any problems that you will have will be fixed there.

12. Warranty. Look at the warranty carefully. Many claim to cover everything, but when you read the fine print you may find that only critical parts such as the drive-train and engine are covered for the full warranty period. Also determine how much you must do in terms of regular maintenance to satisfy the warranty conditions.

TAKE A LONG TEST DRIVE

One of the best ways to try out a new car is to rent one for a day or a week. In addition to rental agencies, many car dealers will also rent. Talk about hands on! If you are considering a late-model used car, you might try the rental agencies that deal in these cars such as Rent-A-Wreck. After driving the car for a few days, you should have a clear idea of how well it handles, what

A Rental Test Drive Could Have Saved a Ton

A friend of ours bought a new car only to find that the steering pulled on her sensitive shoulder. She could not drive it for an extended period of time. She had to trade it in for another car and take a huge loss in the process. If she had done an extended test drive with a rental car, she would have discovered that the steering bothered her shoulder.

quirks it has, and whether you need certain options. Ask the rental agency what problems have occurred with that model. If you are trying to decide between several models, I recommend that you rent each one for a few days and then make up your mind.

While this might sound a bit expensive and time-consuming, you will be buying peace of mind and probably getting a very good deal. This process will make you more relaxed because you will know for certain that you found the best model for your needs. You'll get a good deal because you will know what options you want and don't want.

Buyer Beware

There are dozens of scams which seem to continue year after year. It appears that most scams fall into several broad categories. Dealers charge you for something that is already included in the price such as dealer prep. You see mysterious and bogus charges on your bill such as charges for ADM or DVF, which are charges for virtually nothing. You make a deal, sign the papers, drive out of the lot, and then find that in the fine print it reads "subject to financing." Suddenly you find that your loan is at a much higher interest rate. Some dealers will require you to pay for or buy something that you don't want such as an extended warranty or life insurance. Last but not least, the required white Monroney sticker that should be on the passenger window is missing. This means that you cannot verify that you got the options you are paying for.

As with most purchases, be aware of the extras that are typically offered when buying a new vehicle and know which

Dress Down When Buying Used

When shopping for used cars, wear casual old clothes. You might get a bit dirty looking at the tire treads or rust under the car or leaning into the engine. Never wear a tie or anything loose. Leaning into a running engine with a tie is a recipe for disaster. It could get caught in one of the belts and strangle you.

ones to avoid. Typically these include: fabric conditioning, rust-proofing, undercoating, glazing, and extended warranties. Most experts agree that your new car will do just fine without any of these. Also avoid dealer-installed extras. Anything they install, you can get done later and probably cheaper.

Never buy a used car without checking out the specific history of that car. If you buy any used car, run the make, model, and serial number through CarFax.com. This can tell you if the mileage has been turned back, or if the car has been in an accident or through a flood. If you can contact the previous owner, do it. According to the National Highway Traffic Safety Administration (NHTSA), a significant number of cars have had their mileage turned back, costing the average buyer of such a car over $2,000. In addition some cars have been sold to dealers across state lines to disguise flood damage or that a car was in an accident and repaired.

Never, ever buy a car that has been in an accident. The reason is that the chassis and other important structural elements may have been damaged. These cannot really be repaired. You could find that the tires on your car can never be properly aligned or a number of other permanent problems.

Discount Strategies

Best Single Strategy
Buy a Late-Model Used Car

A late-model used car will cost much less than new and save you on insurance, interest, and taxes. In addition you will be buying a more reliable car if you have bought one with an excellent repair history. A new car does not have a repair history, but with used cars you can be reasonably certain you are getting a reliable model.

A smart used car buyer can save a small fortune over a lifetime. I have mentioned several strategies in this chapter. An additional strategy is to buy the old car from a family who buys a new car regularly. You will get a used car for less than a dealer would charge and the sellers will get more than the dealer would give them on a trade-in.

1. Comparison shopping

By following the steps in the Comparison Shopping section in this chapter, you should be able to locate the lowest retail price for the most reliable and well-designed model with good resale value, low insurance costs, good crash tests, high mpg, and with only those features that you really need.

2. Haggling for a low price

Aim for a 5% profit over the cost of the car to the dealer. This 5% should include any rebates, holdbacks, bonuses, or incentives to the dealership.

With a few exceptions, dealers expect you to haggle over the price. With the help of the Web you should be able to calculate a reasonable figure that a dealer will accept. Make this calculation before you walk into the showroom and bring your notebook with you. You might also bring printouts of pages from Edmunds.com and other car pricing services to back up your offer.

3. Haggling for extras

All those fees that seem to pile up on the final invoice are charges you can haggle about. Ask about every single amount listed. For example, dealers often charge too much for dealer prep. You may be able to negotiate this amount.

4. Custom configurations

If you make a special order, you might also pay less. Since the car does not have to sit on the lot for weeks or months but is passed directly to you, the dealer will save money. Make sure that you get an additional discount as a result.

5. Regular sales

Used cars: February and November.

New cars from current model year; buy after the new-model introduction (NMI): September and October. Ask for an additional 5% discount.

6. Rebates

Car rebates are common as are incentives. Some are given directly to the consumer while others go to the dealer. Dealers can choose to pass along these discounts to the customer or not. Find a dealer who will give you a break.

7. Unusual discounts and sales

When the economy slowed in 2002, many manufacturers offered low or zero percent financing. When a car company is overstocked with certain models, you also might find sweet deals.

8. Internet shopping and mail order

In 2001 about 4% of people purchased a car directly on the Internet according to JD Powers and Associates. During that transaction you will almost certainly talk to a salesperson over the phone who works with Internet buyers. You should be able to shave a bit more off the price this way.

9. Outlet stores and outlet malls

This category does not apply to cars.

10. Closeouts and discontinued models

At the beginning of the new model season, you can get the previous year's models for another 5% off. You will be getting a brand-new car that has not been driven. The very best time to get these is after the new models have been introduced, not before. The reason is that once the new-model introduction (NMI) has begun, the older models become carryovers and the dealer often receives a 5% factory rebate.

11. Floor models, demonstrators, scratch-and-dent, blemished, seconds

There are plenty of cars on the lot that have been driven by customers for test drives or driven regularly by the staff. Ask about these when you make the rounds. It is best to consider a demonstrator as a used car and it should be checked out accordingly.

12. Refurbished

This category does not generally apply to cars.

13. Used

This is the best single strategy for getting a great deal. Please read about this in more detail at the top of this Discount Strategies section.

14. Financing

Used cars and new cars are financed at different interest rates; check with your bank or credit union. Take advantage of special low interest rates offered at dealerships. Be very careful about financing at a used car lot; the interest rate may be much higher than you could get at a bank.

15. Extra discounts

Some energy-efficient cars may qualify for tax credits. Clean fuel and hybrid gas-electric powered cars may get a $2,000 tax deduction. Electric cars might receive a 10% tax credit with a $4,000 maximum. These tax benefits are ending in 2006. As always check the specific tax language before buying. Also you should bear in mind that dealers tend to charge more and haggle less when they know you will get a fat tax break. Don't even mention the tax credit if possible.

Example of combined discounts:

If you bought last seasons (1st discount) demonstrator (2nd discount) after the new models have come out, you could expect two discounts.

Making the Deal

Since there are so many aspects to buying a car, it is easy to get confused. Make sure that everything you have agreed is on paper.

The bottom line is really quite simple: Don't sign anything that you don't understand. Make sure that all charges are spelled out in writing if the dealer requires them. For example, if a dealer insists that you cannot get financing without an extended warranty, have the dealer put this statement in writing. Check the Monroney sticker on your new car to make sure that you got the options you paid for.

After the Sale

If you buy a new car, make sure that you follow all break-in procedures during the break-in period for the new car.

Quite a few states now have Lemon Laws. Essentially these laws state that if your new car that is still under warranty has been repaired unsuccessfully a number of times, you have certain rights. These rights may involve the manufacturer replacing that car, for example. Check with your state attorney general's office for details.

Most warranties will require that you bring your car in for regular maintenance or the warranty will be voided. You need to be aware of what maintenance needs to be done and which shops are authorized to do this work. If you take your vehicle to a nonauthorized garage, you could void your warranty.

Resources

BOOKS

You should be able to find the following books at www.Amazon. com.

For detailed repair histories of automobiles and reviews of new cars buy the most recent edition of:

Consumer Reports Buying Guide, $9.99, Consumer Reports.

Don't Get Taken Every Time: The Ultimate Guide to Buying or Leasing a Car in the Showroom or on the Internet (5th Edition) by Remar Sutton, $14.00, Penguin USA, 2001.

Smart Questions for Savvy Shoppers: The Guide That Gets You the Most for Your Dollar, by Dorothy Leeds with Sharyn Kolberg, $8.99, HarperPaperbacks, 1994.

Newsstand publications:

ConsumerGuide—Car and Truck Test Buying Guide, $9.95, ConsumerGuide Publications.

This book includes reviews, detailed specifications, and a list of other cars in the same category. Extremely useful reference.

Used Car Prices, $6.99, Vehicle Market Research International.

INTERNET

I have created an updated and comprehensive list of useful automobile web sites at the web page for this book at:

www.savvydiscounts.com/thebook

The Federal Trade Commission (FTC) guides to buying a new or used car, financing, renting or leasing:

www.ftc.gov/bcp/conline/edcams/automobiles/index.html

To compare prices of new cars including total costs over an extended period go to Edmunds.com, the authority on new car prices since 1966. This site also includes reviews:

www.edmunds.com

To find the value of your old car both as a trade-in or for sale by yourself go to the Kelly Blue Book site:

www.kbb.com

For crash-test data go to the web site of the Insurance Institute for Highway Safety:

www.hwysafety.org

You can also go to the U.S. Government web site for crash data:

www.nhtsa.dot.gov

To check the mileage and history of a used car, employ the services of CarFax.com:

www.CarFax.com

To get several different loan quotes go to LendingTree.com for both new and used cars:

www.lendingtree.com

Major car sites:

www.chrysler.com

www.ford.com

www.generalmotors.com

www.hondacars.com

www.nissanusa.com

www.toyota.com

If you want to check out a major used car dealer online, try CarMax.com:

www.CarMax.com

To rent a car for an extended test drive try these web sites: For new cars try:

www.alamo.com

www.avis.com

www.hertz.com

For used cars try:

www.rentawreck.com

Search the archives of newsgroups for letters relating to service or product reliability:

groups.google.com

You can also post questions on the appropriate newsgroup.
To check if there have been any unresolved complaints with a dealer go to the Better Business Bureau site:

www.bbb.com

Computer Crunch 7

Don't Even Think about It
Unless You Can Back It Up

Overview

People often ask me, "I need to get a computer, what should I get?" I don't give them a direct answer. Instead I reply, "What do you want to do with your computer? How important is the work you will be doing?" If you have a clear idea of the tasks you want your computer to accomplish, you won't pay for software and hardware you don't use. These days you can buy a computer configured to your individual needs.

A computer is not like a car. With a car you have a pretty clear idea of where you need to go because you do it regularly throughout the year: You go from home to work, you need space to carry the groceries, you go on camping trips and drive through heavy snow in the winter. But a computer can be many different things. This will be determined as much by the software as the initial hardware. It will be up to you to decide just how to configure it and how to shape it into the kind of machine you need.

To a musician, a computer might be a sophisticated drum machine, a mixing and editing device for various recorded tracks, and a CD burner. To a photographer, the computer might be a photo archive and manager, a digital darkroom, and an interactive gallery. To a writer, the computer might be a note taker, a database manager, a spell checker, a thesaurus, and a desktop publisher. It is very likely that you have a clear notion of some of the things you want it to do and a vague notion of other tasks.

A good rule of thumb is that the initial cost of the computer will be about a third to half of your total cost. After you buy the machine, you will probably want to add more software, a UPS (uninterruptible power supply), and a way to easily back up your data. In addition you may also want to add more memory, another hard drive, and a card for specialized tasks such as video. As you can see, the costs can rise dramatically. No matter how you use your machine, you can count on additional expenses:

Everyone should buy a UPS, because even a momentary loss of power can damage your machine and your data. In addition, a UPS will maintain a constant voltage even though the voltage from your power company fluctuates.

You should get a desk and other furniture just for the computer. It is critical that your work area be comfortable and designed for your body. If you type for hours at a computer, a few inches can make the difference between feeling comfortable or uncomfortable. Probably the most important piece of furniture is a solid adjustable office chair with casters that lets you adjust the height. I recommend office supply stores for these.

Just as important is the question of how important is the work you are doing on the computer. The more important and critical your work, the more care should be taken in backing up your precious data. I believe that most people should have a simple way to back up all data on a regular basis. For example, an inexpensive piece of software called Second Copy will allow you to automatically back up your data to a number of devices including a second hard drive, an auxiliary hard drive, or a CD. Once it is set up, it only takes seconds or at most a few minutes to back up your most recent data.

I strongly recommend a second hard drive that connects through the USB port. These are available in standard sizes and can be connected to another computer if your computer crashes. This means that all your data could be available to you on a different machine in case of an emergency. Naturally you will have to have the appropriate software.

If your data is very important, you should back it up to two devices daily. This sounds like a lot of work, but once the software and hardware are configured, it is almost effortless. I back up my data after every sit-down session with the computer and it takes about a minute or two to simply add the new data to the back-up devices.

So here are the principle questions to ask:

- What do I want the computer to accomplish?

- What software will I need to use and/or buy?

- How much data will I create and how much storage space will be needed?

- Do I plan on adding hardware down the road?

- How important is my data?

- How many copies should I keep, and what hardware and software do I need to back it up?

- Do I have a way to access the data if my computer crashes?

What Buyers Need to Know

General Terms

CD-R and CD-RW: for storage, CDs come in two types. There are CDs (CD-RW) where data can be stored and erased and less expensive CDs (CD-R) that only allow you to store data but not erase and reuse that space. You will need a special CD drive and software to save information on these CD disks.

CPU: CPU stands for central processing unit. This is the guts of any computer, the chip that does all the calculating and crunching of data. The faster the CPU the more quickly your computer functions. Speeds are measured in Gigahertz (GHz). You will pay a lot more for a very fast state-of-the-art CPU. I think your money will be better spent adding a second hard drive or more memory.

Data: Data is a very broad term that can refer to all programs, pictures, and notes that are on your computer or more specifically to just the information that you create. All data is stored on a storage device in the form of computer files. The data that you create is probably the most important and precious commodity that you have on your computer. While programs and even computers can be replaced, your data cannot unless you have a backup. Sooner or later you will run into a glitch and lose data.

Hard drive: Probably the most common storage medium is a hard drive. Just about all desktop and large portable computers have one of these built in. You may not be aware of it because it is hidden deep inside the machine. Physically it is a hard disk, which turns very fast with a magnetic medium on the surface. It can store and retrieve information quickly. A hard drive will hold a ton of your data along with the software you use. Hard drive storage is now measured in gigabytes. As I said earlier I strongly recommend that you have a second hard drive which you use to back up your data. Today you can buy an auxiliary drive and plug it into the computer, using the USB port that comes with most machines.

IBM compatible: Most computers these days conform to the IBM standard; this is the most common computer and generally what a consumer will be buying. These are made by a variety of manufacturers including IBM such as Dell, Gateway, Toshiba, Sony, Compaq, and HP.

Macintosh: A computer made by Apple, the Mac now sells less than 5% of the computers made. It is excellent for graphics and desktop publishing. (Most comments made in this chapter will apply to both the IBM and the Mac unless there is a specific reference to the Windows operating system which is just for the IBM standard.)

Operating system: The operating system is the most basic software. It loads into the computer automatically during setup and allows all the other software to run properly. Windows is the most common operating system for the IBM compatible PC. There are many different versions of Windows including Windows 95, Windows 98, Windows 2000, Windows Millennium, Windows XP, and Windows NT. It is quite important to know exactly which version your computer runs and even the revision number of that software.

Can You Buy Too Big a Hard Drive?

How big should your hard drive be? The bigger the better. With larger files like digital photographs, storage is going to become very important. Believe me, you will never be sorry that you paid a bit extra for a large drive. The old joke goes that you can never be too rich or too thin. With computers, you can never have too much RAM memory or too big a hard drive.

RAM: stands for Random Access Memory. Memory is usually in megabytes (MB) or gigabytes (GB). When you are doing work on a computer and creating new data, you are using this very fast but volatile memory. Volatile means that the data only exists as long as the power is on or the computer does not crash. If either of these happens, you will lose your data.

ROM: stands for Read Only Memory such as a standard CD. This is quite different from RAM but the similarity in terms can be confusing.

Storage: Storage refers to the medium on which the data is stored in a non-volatile format. There are a variety of storage methods and devices such as hard drives, a writable CD known as a CD-R, a rewritable CD known as a CD-RW, floppy disks, memory cards, and even storage on the Internet. When a storage device retrieves data it loads it into RAM memory. When it stores data, it saves it in a non-volatile format that keeps your data safe even when the computer is turned off.

Ports

Parallel: Your printer will generally be connected permanently through this port.

PC: This port is used for connecting the mouse.

Serial: Modems, some mice and other devices can connect via this port which is slower than either a parallel or USB port but is still essential because so many devices can use it.

USB: You should not consider a computer without at least one USB port, preferably two. These ports allow you to plug devices into your computer while it is running. Serial and parallel ports generally require that the device already be attached before the computer is turned on. Today a variety of devices can be hooked into the computer via USB such as scanners, auxiliary hard drives, and digital camera transfer cables.

Internet Related

Modem: The modem is a device that connects your computer to the phone line and the Internet. It is often built into the computer these days, but can be added as a separate outside device. I prefer to have it outside the computer because the multiple flashing lights give me a lot more information about the Internet connection than the bare bones blinking in the desktop icon.

Other Peripherals

CD or DVD player: A CD and DVD player can operate like a regular home CD player but in addition can contain programs that can be installed on your computer, or data such as photographs or a searchable encyclopedia and other multimedia. A standard CD or DVD is a ROM device, meaning that the computer can read information from a disk but cannot save information on the disk. A DVD player can read a CD or a DVD; a CD player can only read a CD.

Monitor: You can buy a monitor capable of various resolutions. The dots per inch (dpi) determine the maximum resolution and the dot pitch determines the sharpness.

Sound card: A sound card will allow you to play stereo sound. If sound quality is important to you, you might want to invest in a high-end card.

Other

Laptops: Because these portables are compact, you will have to accept a ready-made configuration. With laptops you should be especially careful to do your homework. They are hard to upgrade and even adding memory can be a daunting chore.

Tower: It seems that most IBM-compatible computers come in a tower case. This was not always so. Flat desktop computers used to be common. Towers are far superior if you need to open the case and add a card, more memory, or another drive. I highly recommend them.

Labeling

Energy Star label: Look for the distinctive Energy Star label for maximum energy savings. Products in the computer category covered in this book include computers, monitors, printers, scanners, and multifunction devices.

Before Shopping

If you are familiar with computers, you should read the local newspaper and check on the Internet for various standard configurations. There are a lot of abbreviations in advertisements, and you should be familiar with these before you walk into a store or finalize a purchase over the Internet. A fairly standard description in a newspaper ad might read like this:

"Intel Pentium 4 processor 2GHz, 512MB ram, CD-RW drive, DVD-Rom drive, 80GB HD, internal modem, 2 USB."

Translation:

This ad is for an IBM compatible computer.

The CPU is an Intel Pentium 4 processor which runs at 2 gigahertz.

The memory is 512 megabytes of random access memory.

There is a rewritable CD drive.

There is also a DVD drive, which is read only (ROM), meaning that it can play CDs and DVDs but you cannot store data on this drive.

Don't Take Specifi- cations for Granted

I bought a computer on the recommendation of a salesman only to find that there was no way to plug a musical keyboard into the sound card. This was a very odd configuration to say the least. My lack of curiosity cost me the price of a separate sound card that I had to install.

There is an 80 gigabyte hard drive.

A modem is built into the computer.

There are two USB ports.

What is almost as interesting about this standard description is what has been left out. You will need to ask and write down the following:

Does it have a serial port? More than one?

Does it have a parallel port? More than one?

Does it have a mouse port?

Does it have a game port?

What sound capability does it have?

Does it come with a monitor?

Does it come with speakers?

Does it come with a printer?

What is the operating system? Which version?

Does it come with other software?

How many expansion slots does it have?

Most manufacturers should be able to supply you with full specifications, known as a spec sheet. On the Internet you can look up and print out a detailed list of specifications. If you have trouble understanding this, you should consult your local young computer nerd. Kids seem to understand this stuff better than adults, so if you can swallow your pride, you might ask a savvy teenager for help.

Comparison Shopping

If you can do a hands-on trial of a computer and software, I highly recommend it. Try out a friend's machine, rent one for an hour at the local Internet cafe, or work with a desktop publishing program at a local copy shop such as Kinkos. Try out a setup at Circuit City or another store that will let you tinker with a display model. I would also cut out several newspaper advertisements and print out Internet offers. Make sure that specifications are listed, so you can compare prices and capabilities.

Learning a Machine Before You Buy

Way back when, in the ancient days of 8-bit computers and when Radio Shack was a major player, I was shopping around for my first computer. The salesman at the RS store let me play with the Radio Shack Color Computer for hours. I came back two days later and played some more. At the end of the day, he had made a sale and in the process I had learned a lot about computers and also felt comfortable with this particular machine.

You should also check the reputations of different manufacturers. If you look for "company name" and "complaint" in discussion groups known as newsgroups, you might get some idea of how a company handles its customers. See the Resources section at the end of this chapter.

Buyer Beware

Avoid those juicy offers of tons of wonderful software. Buying a prepackaged configuration can be costly. While it might look like a good deal on the surface, you may find that you are stuck with a bunch of useless software that is hard to get rid of. Uninstalling software should be simple, but it often isn't. Plus, some "free" software is a bare-bones version of the real thing and often useless—you will have to pay extra to get the full-blown version. In addition, the software you don't use can interfere with the stuff you really need. Unless you can find a computer configuration with most of the software you want at a good price, I suggest that you try to get one with only the operating system, such as Windows.

Don't get a "free" printer or scanner or other equipment unless you need it. The scanner or printer is not really free; it is

Toll Free Service?

A friend of ours made three calls to her computer manufacturer to resolve a problem with standard software that had come installed on the machine. She was told repeatedly to reinstall the software, which she did. It did not solve the problem. Finally a tech support person admitted that he had no idea what was causing the problem.

added into the price you are paying. Instead of getting a "free" printer that you don't need, ask the salesperson for a discount on the computer without the free printer.

Beware of warranties with asterisks*. You will often be presented with a wonderful warranty promising "on-site repair service" followed by an asterisk. When you read the paragraph that the asterisk refers to (if you can find it), it will say something like "some limitations may apply." It could turn out that the "on-site repair service" is only good in some areas and under some conditions. If you open the tower to add another card or hard drive, you might void the warranty.

24/7 customer service sounds good, but often the people you talk to know next to nothing. They seem to know even less at night and on the weekends, so don't count on a lot of help.

Watch out for rebates. Rebates are common in the computer industry. Never buy a computer because of the rebate. While you can save a substantial amount of money, getting that check mailed to you could be a major hassle. The *Wall Street Journal* (6/11/2002) reported that a major computer company, "initially turned down more that 25% of applicants for a $100 rebate on its . . . laptop because they failed to meet one or more of the conditions." To read more about the hassle of rebates go to the Introduction.

Discount Strategies

Best Single Strategy
Buy a Computer As a Custom Configuration

If you can find a local store with a good reputation that has been in business for years, get them to build you a computer to your

An Example of a Custom Configuration

After putting up with standard computers that always had some basic flaw, I decided to ask a local computer man to build me one. In 2000 I ordered a computer with two very large hard drives, two CD drives—a CD and a CD-RW—two USB ports, two serial ports, two parallel ports, and a video card. I did not want any software except for the basic operating system. Nowadays, much of what I requested is standard. But if I had not bought a custom configuration, I could not have bought all this at the time.

specifications. You will get exactly what you want and also the benefit of service after the sale. Plus, you will save a bundle. Make sure your computer is constructed with brand-name components.

Unlike a national company, each local computer business is different. If it has a good reputation, it deserves serious consideration. I think that once you realize that you can get exactly what you want and avoid paying for extras you don't need, the savings will be considerable. I wrote this book with a custom-built computer. It was built to my specs, burned-in before it arrived, and delivered to my door for about $500 less than I would have paid elsewhere at the time.

1. Comparison shopping

By following the steps in the Comparison Shopping section in this chapter, you should be able to locate the lowest retail price for the most reliable and well-designed model with only those features that you really need. I recommend buying name-brand merchandise from authorized dealers. Even if you have a computer custom built, use only brand-name components.

Excellent Local Repair Service

Buying from a local company has numerous advantages. A year and a half after I had my computer built for me locally, I saw an occasional message saying that there was a "boot drive failure." This could have been very serious if it meant that the hard drive had gone bad. Fortunately restarting the computer always worked. Because I had bought from the local company, the technician came to my house to check. We decided to replace the hard drive. At his business he made a perfect copy of the old drive onto a much larger new drive. Then he swapped the bad drive for the good one. I was without my computer for only 24 hours and the total cost to me was about $150. I even got a bigger drive in the bargain.

2. Haggling for a low price

While the price of a new computer is often set, you should haggle if you buy additional equipment as well such as a monitor or printer. It never hurts to ask. You may be able to haggle better over the phone with an online company than a local discount store.

3. Haggling for extras

A local computer store might throw in an accessory for free. The more you spend, the more you should ask.

4. Custom configurations

This is the best single strategy for getting a great deal. Please read about this in more detail at the top of the Discount Strategies section.

5. Regular sales

February.

Computer sales are seasonal. More are sold in the fall and winter than in the spring and summer. Avoid buying around Christmas.

6. Rebates

You will find rebates on a regular basis for computers and computer equipment. The savings can be substantial. Some office supply stores put rebate offers in a special section or on a bulletin board. See our advice about rebates on page 28.

7. Unusual discounts and sales

With the slowdown in sales in the fall of 2002, one major store was offering 0% financing on computers. When the economy is bad, you may notice a number of special deals that are not normally available. Some manufacturers will put you on their special offer e-mail list. Internet and mail order companies have regular offers of free shipping during slow periods.

8. Internet shopping and mail order

Just about all major computer companies now will sell directly to you on the Internet. You may find some deals that are only available on the web. Look also for discount authorized dealers that sell computers and peripherals.

9. Outlet stores and outlet malls

While computers are not commonly sold at brick-and-mortar outlets, you can find quite a few online factory outlets. You may find a variety of discounted new products. Large manufacturers often have their own online factory outlet. Check their web sites.

You can find an updated listing of businesses that have special offers and/or sell directly to the public at:

www.eoutletcenter.com

10. Closeouts and discontinued models

Major manufacturers may have clearance, specials, and closeout items. IBM and Dell, for example, have special sections on their sites for such offers.

11. Floor models, demonstrators, scratch-and-dent, blemished, seconds

All those store demonstration products must be gotten rid of eventually. Ask at stores that have large displays. Office supply stores seem like an especially good place to look; in my experience they will deal with you.

12. Refurbished

Many major manufacturers will sell refurbished computers from their sites. Hewlett-Packard, for example, has a factory outlet division on its web site where it sells refurbished equipment, as does Dell. Dell offers the same warranty and service for refurbished as for new. If you buy refurbished from an unfamiliar company, always check out its reputation, years in business, return policy, and warranty.

I have bought several refurbished computers and found them to be excellent bargains. You can buy current technology at a discount. If the refurbished item comes with only a 30- or 90-day warranty, however, buying an extended warranty might be justified.

129

13. Used

If you have limited needs, used computers can be a very good deal. You can get last-year's technology for much less than today's. For simple word processing, data base collection, and spread-sheet applications, an older Windows or even a DOS machine can be had for almost nothing. Make sure that it comes with a 30-day return.

For most people, a used computer is not a good idea. The requirements of the Internet, digital photography, and desktop publishing just seem to grow and grow. If you plan to use current software, don't use an older machine. You're just asking for trouble.

14. Financing

Look for special financing deals especially during the slow months after Christmas. Businesses that buy large setups should be able to arrange favorable terms.

15. Extra discounts

The price of computers and computer peripherals keeps dropping. The longer you wait, the cheaper they get. If you don't have a crying need for one, take your time. For example, if you think you might get a computer in the fall but wait until the spring, you could save several hundred dollars.

Example of combined discounts:

Buying a floor model (1st discount) in February or later in the spring when regular sales occur (2nd discount) should get you two discounts at the same time.

Making the Deal

When you finally decide to buy, get a detailed printout of the specifications, the warranty, and the cost of each item. Read them before you buy. Ask the dealer or the company, if you are buying direct, about their return policy. More and more companies are imposing a restocking fee, meaning that you could pay a penalty, often around 15%, for returning a computer for a refund.

After the Sale

I recommend that you already have a place ready for your computer at your home. If you are replacing an older computer, you will need to decide what to do with that machine before you bring the new beast home. Once you have the computer in your space, set it up quickly but carefully. Do not wait.

Leave the computer on for at least 24 hours straight. This "burn-in" period will often reveal any problems immediately so that you can return or exchange it promptly before you have done too much work. When you do get your computer up and running, make sure that it is as advertised. I would advise you to make a checklist on a large notepad.

Verify that the hard drive is the size specified. In Windows you can check this with Microsoft Explorer. Right click the Start button, click on Explore, right click on the Drive C icon, then choose Properties. The properties display will give you the size of your drive. In a similar manner make sure that all promised software is either included or is installed.

After the burn-in period you should run a test of your hard drive. Use the built-in ScanDisk utility in Windows (Programs/

Accessories/System Tools/ScanDisk) to perform a thorough test of your hard drive which includes a surface test. With a large drive this could take most of the night, so you might want to start the test before you go to bed and it should be done by the morning.

Every port and every capability of your machine should be tested. Connect the printer and make sure that it prints okay. Test the modem, the sound card, the mouse port, the USB ports, and the CD drives. The Windows operating system can also tell you if ports and devices are working correctly. Click on the Start button then Settings/Control panel/System/Device manager. Then click on each device listed and click Properties. This last screen will tell you if the device is working properly.

This seems like a lot of work and it is, but it is the only way to make sure that your machine is functioning as it should. This testing phase will also familiarize you with your machine. Before you start adding data and putting important work on your hard drive, you want to be certain that it is working properly.

As we pointed out in the Introduction of this book, you should *not* fill out the warranty card until you can no longer return it to the store where you bought it. Once you fill out the warranty card, you are not dealing with the store and getting a refund or exchange; instead, you are dealing with the manufacturer and getting an item repaired.

Don't Whip Yourself

A month after you have bought your machine, you will almost certainly see an offer that looks like a better one. Don't concern yourself. If you got a good deal at the time and the computer works as advertised, you got a very good bargain.

Resources

BOOKS

Computers will continue to change rapidly so just about any book I list will be out of date. I suggest you turn to online resources.

INTERNET

I have created an updated and comprehensive list of useful computer web sites at the web page for this book at:

www.savvydiscounts.com/thebook

You can go to the U.S. Government's Energy Star site and browse some of the latest energy efficient designs at:

www.energystar.gov

For reviews of computers and peripherals:

www.consumerreview.com

www.consumersearch.com

www.pcmag.com

www.ratings.net

www.reviewboard.com

Major computer companies:

www.dell.com

www.gateway.com

www.hp.com

www.ibm.com

Major computer retailers:

www.bestbuy.com

www.circuitcity.com

www.jandr.com

Try these office supply stores with catalogues and excellent web sites. Some list clearance furniture and technology or have a general clearance center. You will also find online rebate centers:

www.officedepot.com

www.officemax.com

www.quillcorp.com

www.staples.com

www.viking.com

Refurbished and closeouts:

www.eoutletcenter.com
www.hpfactoryoutlet.com

Used computers:

www.usedcomputerrecycling.com

Price comparison:

shopper.cnet.com

www.BizRate.com

www.Dealtime.com

www.PriceGrabber.com

For online opinions:

www.epinions.com

Buy quality backup software. The "Second Copy" software program makes backups a breeze:

www.centered.com

Search the archives of newsgroups for letters relating to service or product reliability:

groups.google.com

You can also post questions on the appropriate newsgroup. To check if there have been any unresolved complaints with a dealer go to the Better Business Bureau site:

www.bbb.com

Exercise Equipment Ecstasy

8

Get Your Butt in Gear Without Paying Through the Nose

Overview

Exercise equipment is often an impulsive purchase. You really want to get those muscles moving, lose some weight, and feel better about yourself. The TV ads may look very enticing: all those happy healthy people showing you how easy it is. For only twenty minutes, three times a week, you will look like Arnold Schwarzenegger.

Now for a reality check. Much if not most equipment ends up in the closet and never gets used. People start with good intentions but cannot keep up. Spending a lot of money is not as important as finding the right equipment that you enjoy using and that you can stick with. How much you like and use a particular exercise machine is more personal and more individual than just about any other product category included in this book.

And remember all those barely used exercise machines that

ended up in storage. You can probably get these for as much as 75% off by looking in the classified ads in your local newspaper.

Here are some of the major personal considerations:

1. Your age, your health, your level of fitness

You should always consult your doctor before starting an exercise program. Rowing machines can harm people with bad backs, for example. If you have not been exercising, you will want a machine that will let you get into shape very gradually. You may want to make sure that your heart rate does not go over the proper level.

2. Your individual needs

Your height, weight, sense of balance, and your boredom threshold are important considerations. Some people feel unstable using skiing machines or standing on the moving platform of a treadmill. Boredom is a major consideration. Many people prefer a health club because being around other people eliminates monotony. You may find that listening to music or watching TV is all it takes to keep you from becoming bored, yet certain machines may turn you off more than others.

3. Cost

You can spend $100 on a simple stationary bicycle to over $5,000 for a treadmill. In between there are a myriad of choices. Buying top quality is not the most important consideration. While you should pay for good sturdy equipment, the machine needs to be something that you feel comfortable with. Paying $5,000 for a machine that you rarely use, is not a good buy. If you buy such a device and never use it, you are not only getting fatter but poorer.

KEEP IN MIND THESE EXERCISE BASICS:

The best exercise is the one that you can stick to.

You might want to vary your routine so that you walk or jog one day and do aerobic dancing or ride an exercise bicycle another day. In fact, experts often recommend, for both health and psychological reasons, that you vary your exercise from day to day. Giving your muscles a day's rest after a workout on a resistance machine is often a good idea.

Start slowly. Get into the habit of doing warm-ups and cooldowns at the start and end of your workout. If you injure yourself in the beginning, it is unlikely that you will be motivated to begin again after you recover. Get a good book on exercise and read it. The right warm-ups, stretching, breathing, and methods for gradually increasing your exercise level are all critical for good health and avoiding injury.

WHAT YOU NEED FROM EXERCISE:

There are three main goals to exercise as told to me by my doctor: flexibility, strength, and endurance. It is unlikely that just one exercise will give you all three.

In addition to your aerobic (endurance) exercise you should stretch (flexibility). You should also lift some small weights (strength/isotonic) or use a resistance device that lets you work your muscles against flexible rods or rubber bands. Some skiing machines work both the upper and lower body at the same time as do some stationary bikes, giving you both an aerobic and isotonic workout.

Even if you decide to start with an aerobic machine such as a treadmill or bicycle, you might want to own a few small weights (dumbbells) in different sizes. Recent studies have shown that even elderly people will gain significant benefits from mild

Small Weights Really, Really Work

I resisted using weights, even after being advised by my doctor to do so. When I finally got into the habit, I found that many of the muscle problems involved with using a computer keyboard were much improved. Even my back was better. So as a recovering couch potato, I can attest to the effectiveness of working out with very light dumbbells several times a week.

weight lifting. Other studies have shown that this kind of exercise helps women avoid bone loss more effectively than calcium supplements.

I recommend that you have a comfortable nonslip mat for stretching. In addition you should own a copy of the book *Stretching* (see Resources section at the end of this chapter) which has detailed diagrams for stretching and for attaining flexibility.

For starters you do not need to spend a lot of money to get going. A good pair of shoes for walking or jogging, an exercise mat for stretching and using weights, a small set of dumbbells, and a couple of books and/or videos might only run you about $100. Next you might want to add a low-cost exercise machine for rainy days or late-night sessions.

The hard part is to find equipment that you will enjoy using, so consider what sort of activities you already do before making a purchase. If you like to bicycle, a stationary bike might be an ideal way to stay in shape during the cold weather months when you might not want to ride outside. If you enjoy skiing, a ski machine could be a good choice.

What Buyers Need to Know

Because this purchase is so individual and so personal, I recommend that you try out the various types of machines.

The main categories are:

Stair climbers

Aerobic step-up boxes

Stationary bicycles

Skiing machines

Treadmills

Complete home gyms

Weight benches

Rowing machines

DEFINITIONS:

Isotonic and isometric: working muscles against a resistance which results in a significant improvement in muscle tone.

Aerobics: exercise which increases breathing and heart rate for a short period of time.

Endurance: exercising for a sustained period of time usually accomplished with aerobic exercise.

Resistance: used in isotonic exercises; the resistance can be weights or an elastic-type device.

Before Shopping

There are a couple of main considerations for just about any piece of equipment and a number of minor ones.

1. The equipment should be very sturdy. You are going to be putting the full weight of your body in motion so it needs to be well constructed. When possible test out the equipment in the store and make sure that you feel secure.

2. The motion should be smooth and easy, not jerky. Stationary bicycles, rowing machines, and skiing machines will move more smoothly with a weighted metal flywheel.

3. It should be easily adjustable. Some treadmills require you to get off the device to reset the incline, while others can raise and lower the incline from the exercise position.

4. Some are much noisier than others. Certain models of skiing machines and treadmills make a lot of racket.

5. Consider how much space you have. Exercise bikes tend to be fairly compact while a home gym can take up half a room but does make a great clothes rack. Ideally you want something that you do not have to set up and collapse each time. While the salespeople will tell you that it is easy, it can just become one more impediment to exercising. Use a tape measure to determine how much space you can spare before you buy.

6. Monitor the level and intensity of your workout. You will want some gauges to help you track your exercise, such as an MPH gauge on a stationary bicycle. Yet avoid lots of high-tech gadgets and gizmos because these are

not that important, can add a lot to the price, and beyond the basics won't help you get a better workout.

7. Consider the weight. I have a fairly light exercise bicycle which is easy to store on one side of the room and then move into the middle for a workout. This versatility adds to its usefulness. Big, heavy equipment must be carefully positioned and incorporated into your home because once it is in place, you probably won't relocate it.

8. Is assembly required? Some home gyms can take up to five hours to put together. Make sure you have a spare day on a weekend to do this. Frankly I would avoid anything that takes this much time unless you are certain of its value. If you need to return it, you will have to disassemble it.

9. Can you return equipment you don't like? Just like any other purchase, you should return stuff for a refund if it does not meet your needs. However, this category by its very nature is heavy, cumbersome, and not easy to return.

Comparison Shopping

Different people will respond better to different exercises and the only way to find out, is to do a hands-on test of various machines.

To get a good sense of the kind of equipment that is now available and also whether you will enjoy using it, I suggest that you get a day pass to a local health club. There are a number of ways to do this. Some clubs will let you pay by the day if you live more than a certain number of miles from the club. Others will let you try out the club for one day before you sign up with a long-term contract. Your employer may have an exercise room or a free deal with a health club. Alumni and alumnae who live near their college or university may find that they can use the facilities for little or no cost.

If you cannot get a day pass, ask to be shown around the club by pros who can explain all the equipment to you. They should be glad to do this, since it may mean that they can sell you a membership. In addition there is a chain of stores that specializes in selling new and used athletic devices. Play It Again Sports lets you compare new and used equipment side by side.

Large discount department stores such as Wal-Mart sell a variety of equipment and you should check these out. The advantage is that you can examine the products there without a salesman trying to pressure you into making a purchase.

Avoid buying a device you see advertised on TV. First of all, if it is really good, it will be popular and if it is popular, you should be able to find one used at a big discount. More than that, you usually cannot try a machine shown in an infomercial on TV.

You can look at a number of machines on the Internet. Nautilus, NordicTrack, and Bowflex all have web sites. See the Resources section at the end of this chapter for web addresses.

Buyer Beware

This equipment really needs a longer trial period than others mentioned in this book. You need to be able to return this simply if you do not like it and you need a reasonable amount of time to try it out before returning. I would suggest that a 30-day return policy should be the minimum, while 60 or 90 days would be even better.

Discount Strategies

Best Buying Strategies
Buy Exercise Equipment Used

There is a great selection of used exercise equipment at cut-rate prices, so the best single strategy award goes to buying used equipment. Look for ads in local classifieds, check the Internet or eBay and also at stores such as Play It Again Sports that sell both new and used goods. You can compare used prices on eBay.

Build Your Own Custom Gym Slowly

You can own an exercise bench with small weights for around $100, and you can buy an exercise bicycle for about the same amount. Before spending hundreds or thousands of dollars, it might make sense to try a low-cost unit. If you use it and can stick to the exercise regimen, then you should consider getting something more robust.

Starting Small

We bought an inexpensive exercise bicycle for less than $100 many years ago and it has worked quite well. When it finally dies, I probably will get a more expensive one with a heavy flywheel now that I know we will use it regularly.

145

1. Comparison shopping

By following the steps in the Comparison Shopping section in this chapter, you should be able to locate the lowest retail price for the most reliable and well-designed model with only those features that you really need.

Don't forget to compare used prices as well. Check the classifieds in your local newspapers. You may be able to find exactly what you want in mint condition for a used price. At a Play It Again Sports store you may be able to compare new and used equipment side by side.

2. Haggling for a low price

If you buy used equipment from an individual, you should consider the asking price to be negotiable. This holds true at a used-equipment store as well.

3. Haggling for extras

If you are buying an exercise machine, ask if the store will throw in a set of dumbbells or a mat or a video for free.

4. Custom configurations

As I recommend, you can design your own gym one step at a time. With this slow approach you will get a better sense of what you like to do and what works best for you.

5. Regular sales

February

6. Rebates

Look for rebates on the Internet from the various manufacturers. A search in google.com for "rebates exercise equipment" should bring up the latest rebate offers.

7. Unusual discounts and sales

During a slow economy look for special sales, discounts, and financing. Some manufacturers will put you on their special offer e-mail list. Check their web sites.

8. Internet shopping and mail order

As always, if you know exactly what you want, you can save a considerable amount on new equipment by buying directly from the manufacturer or from a discount sports web site. You should be able to find quite a range of used equipment on eBay as well.

9. Outlet stores and outlet malls

While a few brick-and-mortar outlet stores may stock equipment, you can find numerous factory outlets on the Internet that will sell equipment directly to the consumer. A search in google.com for "discount outlets exercise equipment" should bring up these online stores.

10. Closeouts and discontinued models

Look for these at the end of the season in early spring and before the new season has begun in the fall.

11. Floor models, demonstrators, scratch-and-dent, blemished, seconds

At the end of the season look for these at large department stores and other places that carry exercise equipment during the winter months.

12. Refurbished

This does not generally apply to this category.

13. Used

This is one of two strategies for getting a great deal. Please read about this in more detail at the top of this Discount Strategies section.

14. Financing

A low-interest credit card might be appropriate for this kind of purchase. Pay more than the minimum so that you can pay it off quickly. Some manufacturers and stores may offer their own financing but it will generally be more expensive. If you are offered a no-interest or no-payments deal for 6 to 12 months, ask for a discount if you pay cash.

15. Extra discounts

If you buy an exercise bike and a set of dumbbells ask for a discount.

Example of combined discounts:

Buying a floor model (1st discount) at the end of the season (2nd discount) should get you a great double discount.

Making the Deal

If the product is going to be shipped, get a complete itemized invoice with the make, model number, and color if applicable plus any extras and the cost for each. Make sure that it also includes shipping charges, taxes, and the projected date that your new equipment will arrive.

If you put the order on a credit card, ask that your card not be charged until the item is shipped. You should not have to be paying for something that has been back ordered and not yet available.

When the equipment arrives, make sure that you got what you ordered and that all the parts and pieces are in the package. The instructions both for assembly and use are very important.

After the Sale

Like all new purchases, you should assemble and set up your new exercise set as soon as possible. You want to make sure that it works properly. However, since you are bound to be a bit out of shape, you should not try to ride your new stationary bike, for example, at full tilt. While this would be a good way to test the equipment, it could cause an injury. The best strategy is to start your regular routine ASAP and gradually work your way up to a full workout. While you probably won't be stressing your equipment to its maximum in time for a return of the equipment, you will have worked it enough that most defects will appear.

In addition, you will need to know how to use the device properly. If you use exercise equipment in the wrong way, you can do a lot of damage. Although you may not hurt yourself, you could get into the habit of doing an exercise incorrectly and negate all the benefits. Read the manual even if it goes against your nature. It is critical that you read the directions carefully, ask the pro at the health club for advice, and look at the video that may have come with the machine.

Bottom line, if you find that your back hurts after exercising or that some muscle is out of whack, make sure that you are going through the motions in the right way.

Resources

BOOKS

You should be able to find the following books at www. Amazon.com.

> *Stretching: 20th Anniversary* by Bob Anderson and Jean Anderson, $15.95, Shelter Publications, 2000.

> *Smart Questions for Savvy Shoppers: The Guide That Gets You the Most for Your Dollar,* by Dorothy Leeds with Sharyn Kolberg, $8.99, HarperPaperbacks, 1994.

INTERNET

I have created an updated and comprehensive list of useful exercise equipment web sites at the web page for this book at:

> *www.savvydiscounts.com/thebook*

Web addresses of well-known fitness equipment companies:

www.ballystore.com	*www.nordictrack.com*
www.bowflex.com	*www.proform.com*
www.nautilusfitnessproducts.com	*www.totalgym.com*

Buy, sell, and trade sports equipment at Play It Again Sports stores. Both new and used equipment are available plus a store locater:

> *www.playitagainsports.com*

Explanations and listings of home fitness equipment:

www.fitness-equipment-101.com

Reviews and feedback on equipment:

www.epinions.com

Search the archives of newsgroups for letters relating to service or product reliability:

groups.google.com

You can also post questions on the appropriate newsgroup. To check if there have been any unresolved complaints with a dealer go to the Better Business Bureau site:

www.bbb.com

Furniture Frustrations 9

It Looked Good in the Showroom So Why Is It Different in My House?

Overview

You can spend thousands of dollars on just the right sofa with the perfect fabric or fifty dollars for a yard sale couch in good condition. The fifty-dollar couch will last for years and the kids can jump on it.

There is more variation in price with furniture than just about any category in this book. The choice is up to you how much you want to spend. In addition there are dozens of major furniture manufacturers that often make hundreds of different pieces that can be covered or finished in hundreds of different ways. The number of choices is mind-boggling.

You live with your furniture every day. Finding the right cabinet that goes with the furniture you already own could cost a lot of money and take a bit of time and patience. If you are buying several pieces of furniture, it is even more important that you make sure they fit together. To get the best value you should not be in a hurry.

What Buyers Need to Know

Furniture has hundreds of terms. Learn the jargon for the kind of item you are considering. Wood furniture has one set of terms, upholstered another, and mattresses are in their own world. Here are just a few examples to get you started.

GENERAL TERMS:

Case goods: these include cabinets, tables, desks, chests.

Dovetail joints: interlocking joints that join pieces of wood together. Look for these in quality construction of case goods, especially drawers.

Kit furniture: quality components you put together and finish yourself, so you save a lot of money.

RTA or ready-to-assemble: also known as "knock-down" these easy to put together furniture sets will save you money because you do much of the work plus they are easier to ship.

Upholstered: furniture that has an outer cover of fabric, vinyl, leather or other material that often covers filling, padding, stuffing and/or springs.

Veneer: a thin layer of attractive and/or expensive wood that covers the material underneath.

Avoid Deception by Reading the Label

There is a lot of deception in the furniture industry. Much of this has to do with either mislabeling or labeling in such a way to give the impression that a piece of furniture is something that it is not. Unfortunately, this means that you must pay close attention to the manufacturer's descriptions of furniture and make sure that you are getting what you are paying for.

With the help of information from the Federal Trade Commission (FTC) I have put together definitions of some of these basic and often confusing terms.

Color or grain design finish: This is a color or stain applied to the wood. When using wood names for the finish, manufacturers must state that the finish was applied and it does not refer to the wood itself. For example, the term "walnut finish" is not correct, but the term "walnut color" or "walnut finish on walnut veneers and selected solid hardwoods" would be acceptable.

Imitation leather: It is illegal to give the impression that a covering is genuine leather when it is not.

Origin of furniture: So many furniture styles are labeled Spanish or Danish you might think the furniture came from these countries. However, much of these sold in the U.S. are made in the U.S. When confusion or deception could occur, furniture must state clearly the country of origin in which the furniture was made.

Outer covering: Labels on upholstered coverings must state the mixture of materials used such as "55% Cotton, 45% Rayon" and include any materials that make up the covering.

Simulated or imitation: Imitation wood abounds. Simulated wood grain is also common. Furniture cannot be labeled in such a way that the simulation or imitation is misrepresented. For example, the FTC says about materials simulating wood, "No wood names should be used to describe any materials simulating wood without disclosures making it clear that the wood names used are merely descriptive of the color and/or grain design or other simulated finish; nor should any trade names or coined names be employed which may suggest that such materials are some kind of wood."

Solid wood construction: This means that all of the exposed surfaces are constructed of solid wood of the type named. If more than one type of solid wood is used and one of the woods is named, then all of the principal woods should be disclosed. In place of naming the specific woods, a general designation of the type of wood, such as "hardwood" or "softwood" may be used.

Stuffing, filling, padding: These materials are used in upholstered furniture and must be truthfully labeled.

Wood products: These are artificially created wood boards made from wood particles or fibers such as "hardboard," "particleboard," "chipcore," or "fiberboard." Some labels may just use the general name "wood products."

Before Shopping

The better you can visualize how a new piece of furniture will fit into your room, the happier you will be with your purchase. The most important item you will need is a quality tape measure. Measure the space where the new piece will go. If possible put some cardboard boxes in that space to closely approximate its size. Another method is to put some masking tape on the floor to mark out the size of a new piece that you are considering. Walk around the masking tape as if the new furniture were there. How does it feel? Should it be smaller or larger or in a different part of the room?

In addition to a tape measure, you should buy some graph paper and do a simple drawing of the room to scale. Mark where the new or replacement piece will go. I also recommend that you take several photographs of the room and take these with you when you shop. In the store it is easy to get distracted by a sales pitch and a particularly comfortable couch. The photograph of your room will bring you back to reality.

If you are trying to find furniture to go with a certain color scheme, bring a swatch of fabric that is the same color. You might be able to find a bit of cloth you can snip from underneath a couch, or you can print out the color on your computer if you can get it close. Take these color samples with you to the showroom. If you custom order a new couch with a specific fabric, you will not be able to return the furniture if the color is wrong. In this case the burden is on you to make sure that the fabric and color you choose is the right one. Also be aware that color is relative. A blue couch next to a yellow rug in the showroom might appear to be a different shade of blue next to a red rug in your home.

The more you can do before you go to a furniture store the better. Get several furniture catalogues from major manufacturers, check furniture stores on the Internet, get catalogues of furniture kits, or collect furniture inserts in the Sunday newspaper. See the Resources section at the end of this chapter for web addresses. Read the descriptions in detail and check all the shipping and delivery notices. Get a sense of how the business works

Two for One Futon

Futons are especially versatile. They can be couches or beds or even both. We have owned one for years and use it as a couch in our living room and as a guest bed when needed. They can also be transported easily since the futon and frame can be folded.

so that you can be in a better position to bargain. For example, you might be able to point out that a store on the Internet requires a lower deposit than the local retail store.

In addition to measuring the space for new furniture, you should measure all the doors, stairs, elevators, and hallways that must be negotiated to deliver your new couch. This is your responsibility. If you order a couch and it arrives as promised but it is too large to be moved into your apartment, it is your fault and the money is still due. I suggest that you make a rough plan of the path the new furniture must travel to be carried into your home. Measure each doorway and any obstacles that might be in the way.

Comparison Shopping

Furniture is very hard to compare. With so many manufacturers, styles, finishes, and fabrics there are literally millions of possible combinations. Yet if you spend time looking, you will get a sense of the options that are available. Then you can decide if you need a deluxe model or can do just as well with a less costly one. For example, you could buy an inexpensive mattress for a

Two for One Couch

My mother lived in a small New York apartment for many years. When I came to visit, she unfolded the convertible couch in the living room. Since I was only there for a few weeks during the year, it made sense not to have a full spare guest room that she would have to pay for all year. The bed was quite comfortable.

guest room because the mattress will be used less often and therefore will last a long time. Yet the same mattress for constant everyday use might be a poor choice.

Learn to recognize quality. Well-made upholstered furniture should have fabric and seams that fit precisely and are almost invisible. There is nothing like a hands-on examination. With a cabinet you should open all the doors, slide out drawers and examine how well joints fit together. When you push against an upright cabinet, it should feel stable. A well-made piece works effortlessly while a lower quality piece might need to be jostled at times to get a drawer to go back into place. Screws are preferable to nails especially on the back panel. Hinges need to be strong and sturdy. You should not see glue or fasteners poking out at the joints.

You should go to at least three different showrooms with furniture from different companies. Furniture salespeople are particularly aggressive. They may say things such as, "You must accept this deal today as the price will go back up to the regular price tomorrow!" Simply ignore this. They will take your money tomorrow and may even give you a better deal once you have some comparison prices that you can quote.

Furniture is often sold in suites or sets that might save you money if you really want and need all that matching furniture.

Most new furniture comes with a warranty, some even for life. Check the details for different types of furniture and from different manufacturers.

Consider furniture that does double duty. A relatively inexpensive futon can be a couch or a bed. A convertible sofa can make a spare room into a guest room in a jiffy. In a sense you are getting two items for the price of one.

Buyer Beware

Furniture companies consistently rank in the top five category of consumer complaints nationwide. Slow delivery, no delivery, refusal to give a refund, unauthorized substitutions, misrepresentation of materials, and selling trade-ins as floor models are common.

Check the reputation of the store and how long it has been in business. Although there are plenty of discount chain stores where I live, I prefer the local store that has been in business for over forty years. I have found that this dealer gives me a much better price when all the fees are added in. It not only delivers on time but brings in the new furniture and disposes the old. It does this for a reasonable price. Because I have been a loyal customer, I believe I get a better deal. Other stores appear to have lower prices but when the cost of delivery, setup, and disposal of the old item are factored in, the prices are really no different.

If you are starting to get serious about a coffee table or a bedroom suite, ask about the store's return policy before you get too excited. If the piece is standard and not a custom order, you should be able to return it for a refund. Some stores may only allow an exchange. However, if you order a custom piece with a particular fabric, you probably will not be able to return it.

And what about late deliveries? If the furniture is not delivered within a reasonable amount of time, you should be able to walk away from the deal. Set a target date for delivery and a final date after which you can cancel the entire order.

Pay a small deposit or none if possible. If you pay the full amount with either store credit or a credit card, insist that you not be charged until the furniture is delivered. There are plenty of horror stories about furniture being delayed for months while interest is piling up on a charge made earlier. Special orders typically require a 50% deposit.

Mattresses

Mattresses are a special case when it comes to furniture and can be an incredibly frustrating purchase. Yet unlike most other furniture, a mattress is absolutely essential since you will spend a third of your life in bed.

Manufacturers and stores have deliberately made it hard to comparison shop for mattresses. Some big department stores may have a particular line that is only carried in that store! So it is virtually impossible to compare that line to another made by the same manufacturer in a different store.

Yet there is a way to cut through all this mattress morass. Most mattresses are constructed of coils made of a certain thickness of wire. The more coils, the better and the thicker the wire, the lower the gauge, the better. The number and quality of the coils is important because over time a mattress will sag if these are not adequate. But you might not be able to tell this when you lie down on a new bed in the showroom. To make comparison shopping simple always ask for the number of coils and the gauge of the wire and then lie down on the bed for about ten minutes in the showroom. Also remember that the mattress sits on a box spring which should always be bought at the same time.

When you go shopping wear loose comfortable clothes with shoes that you can take off easily. If you live with someone, bring your partner with you and have him or her dress accordingly. The partner is important because you will need a mattress with plenty of room to move. The average sleeper turns in bed fifty times a night. This means that for both of you to be comfortable you need more than just the space your two bodies will occupy. Also make sure that the bed remains firm and does not slope toward the middle when the two of you are lying down. Virtually all beds are advertised as "firm" so ignore claims that one is firmer than another and instead trust your senses.

Also ignore the flashy ticking, the cloth cover on the mattress. While it looks great in the showroom, you will hardly ever see it since it will be covered with a pad and then a sheet. The ticking is really there for show.

And while you may have trouble comparison shopping, many salespeople have a secret book that does list which mattresses are comparable to which. Try to get a salesperson to show you that book.

Comparison shopping for a mattress can save you a bundle, so it is definitely worth your time. For example, one study found that you could pay $900 or $2,100 for virtually the same mattress; another study found a range of $579 to $1,500 for almost the same bedding.

Mattress terminology:

Box spring: the bedding that supports the mattress

Coils: You are supported by spring coils inside the mattress. Rule of thumb: minimum 300 for a full-sized bed, 375 for a queen, 450 for a king

Gauge: The thickness of the coil, the lower the number the thicker the wire. Rule of thumb: Look for 12¾ to 14 gauge

Ticking: Fabric that covers the mattress

Discount Strategies

Best Buying Strategies
Buy Expensive Furniture By Mail Order/Internet

If you are buying brand-name furniture, especially in a custom configuration, it will be shipped from the factory. So why pay a middleman? Most furniture is made in a small area of North Carolina. You can order directly at wholesale prices through several companies.

Mail-order shopping can save 30% to 60% over the Manufacturer's Suggested Retail Price (MSRP). Like all mail order, you must be certain of the specifications. The more precise you can be, the better. View the pieces you want to buy in showrooms, write down the make and model. You can also look at pictures and descriptions on the Net. Make certain of all the specifications before you order and be sure to keep good records. Some stores require a minimum of $2,000. See the Resources section at the end of this chapter for web addresses.

Buy Used

If you just need solid, serviceable furniture, consider used. One of the truly great deals today is secondhand furniture. For some reason a barely used couch could go for $50 while a new one might cost $500 or more. If you are furnishing a den or a child's playroom, this might be a smart way to buy. If you have the patience, you can find just about anything secondhand. You will often find pieces in old-fashioned styles which are now unavailable and can add a touch of class to a decor. You can see wonderful examples of how to decorate and furnish your home with these items from bygone eras in the *Shabby Chic* book and TV program on the cable STYLE channel. See the Resources section at the end of this chapter.

Yard sales are a gold mine for furniture with prices up to 90% off the new price. A surprising amount of furniture is discarded. One woman furnished much of her apartment by grabbing throwaways and refinishing them. Some stores specialize in used furniture. Check local classified advertisements as well. Always haggle over the price. Avoid yard sales run by dealers.

1. Comparison shopping

By following the steps in the Comparison Shopping section in this chapter, you should be able to locate the lowest retail price for the quality of furniture that you require.

2. Haggling for a low price

Bargaining is standard in furniture and the markup is often 50% or more. Even discount stores have plenty of room to negotiate, so don't feel shy. Bargain hard at a retail store by reminding the salespeople that you can save 30% to 60% over the

Manufacturer's Suggested Retail Price if you order through the mail.

3. Haggling for extras

If you buy more than one item, ask for free delivery, free setup, and free removal of your old furniture. Or ask the retailer to throw in a free chair or rug.

4. Custom configurations

You can custom order just what you want. If this means that you can avoid paying for features you don't want, it could save you money.

5. Regular sales

Furniture: January, February, June, July, August, and September.
   Mattresses: February and June.
   Outdoor furniture: May.

6. Rebates

The major furniture manufacturers may offer rebates. Look for rebates on the Internet from the various manufacturers. A search in google.com for "rebates furniture" should bring up the latest rebate offers.

Don't Forget Office Supply Stores

Office supply stores are an excellent source for desks, computer hutches, and bookcases. Most carry a wide variety at a reasonable cost. You don't normally think of furniture with office supplies, but today's megaoffice stores have quite a selection.

7. Unusual discounts and sales

When the housing market takes a dive, look for sales at furniture stores since these two sectors of the economy are closely linked.

8. Internet shopping and mail order

This is one of two best strategies for getting a great deal. Please read about this in more detail at the top of this Discount Strategies section.

9. Outlet stores and outlet malls

Many stores claim to be furniture outlets, but may not be. Deceptive practices are rampant in the furniture business so check the reputation of the store. However, in North Carolina, close to the furniture industry you will find legitimate clearance and closeout outlets.

10. Closeouts and discontinued models

Styles come and go and last year's popular decor might go for a song this year. Always ask. However, also be very wary. The furniture industry has been known to misrepresent these. A model is legally discontinued when, according to the FTC, "the manufacturer has in fact discontinued its manufacture or the industry member offering it for sale will discontinue offering it entirely after clearance of his existing inventories. . . ."

11. Floor models, demonstrators, scratch-and-dent, blemished, seconds

Furniture showrooms are packed with display models which get changed regularly. In addition, some pieces will be a bit scuffed up. I would ask to see these first, before even considering a brand-new piece.

166

However, just like discontinued models, misrepresentation is common in the industry. The FTC states that "a 'floor sample,' 'demonstration piece,' etc., should not be used to describe 'trade-in,' repossessed, rented or any furniture except that displayed for inspection by prospective purchasers at the place of sale for the purpose of determining their preference and its suitability for their use."

12. Refurbished

Upholstery shops may sell reupholstered items for a lot less than new. If well crafted, the quality should be the same. Call around within your area.

13. Used

This is one of two best strategies for getting a great deal. Please read about this in more detail at the top of this Discount Strategies section.

14. Financing

Many stores will offer 90 days same as cash or no interest for six months. Take advantage of these but read the fine print. Often you will find that if you miss the deadline, you will be paying very high interest from the moment the deal was made. Most furniture stores would love to finance your purchase. You will often pay top dollar for that convenience. Small purchases can be put on a low-interest credit card which may give you more rights as a consumer. Consider a bank loan for a large remodeling project. If you are offered a no interest or no payments deal for 6 to 12 months, ask for a discount if you pay cash.

15. Extra discounts

Kit furniture is a very smart way to get new furniture for a lot less. Modern kits are simple to put together and don't take that much time. Because they are shipped in pieces instead of assembled, you may find that these are easier to deliver to your apartment.

Example of combined discounts:

Get a discontinued (1st discount) furniture kit (2nd discount) for two discounts.

Making the Deal

Get a detailed description of the furniture you are buying. The more information the better—make, model, fabric, wood construction, finish, number of pieces, etc. Make sure that all extra charges are itemized on the invoice such as delivery, setup, and taxes. If you have all the specifications in writing, most companies will abide by those rules. Leave something unspecified and you are inviting trouble.

For example, you may want to forbid any substitutions. This is especially true with mattress sales. You may also want to specify a deadline for delivery of your goods. This means that if your furniture is not delivered by that date, you can get a refund or renegotiate. Be sure to ask if you have been given a complete list of charges and that there are no extra costs.

Make the smallest deposit you can negotiate. Do not pay the full amount until the furniture is delivered. If possible, pay with a credit card. A credit card may give you more legal rights in case there is a problem. If you are dissatisfied, you may be able to dispute the payment with the aid of your credit card company to get a refund. However, once you have paid cash, you will have a much more difficult time getting your money back.

After the Sale

Furniture companies have a reputation for taking longer than planned to deliver your new items. Do not get rid of your old furniture until your new piece has arrived. While it may be a little inconvenient to move your old furniture out the day your new stuff gets there, you will avoid having to sit on the floor when the promised delivery takes weeks longer than anticipated. And never, never, get rid of that old bed until the new one has come unless you like to sleep on the floor.

Never accept delivery until you have had a chance to thoroughly examine your new furniture.

First: Before opening look carefully at the boxes or crates. If you see a cut in the cardboard look for a corresponding cut on the furniture inside. If there is a hole in the cardboard, look for damage close to the area. If you see a significant problem, you can refuse the delivery and have the unopened boxes returned with a notation about the damage.

Second: After the crates are opened, look for scratches, dings, and stains, and make sure everything you ordered is there. For example, make sure that all the chairs were delivered with the dining room table. Take out your swatch of sample fabric and place it on your new couch. Is the fabric the same as the one you ordered? Some furniture might come with extra hardware or a dining room table with an expansion leaf. Check that all extras are included.

Refuse to sign a bill of sale until you are satisfied. Once the delivery truck has left, returning the item can be a major hassle. You may have to pay return shipping and insurance. Horror stories abound about people who accepted delivery of furniture that they then wished to return.

If you happen to get the delivery truck from hell with a driver who insists that he and his team must leave, write the following on the invoice: "subject to inspection" on the bill of sale and then sign. Do this only as a last resort. Ideally you should check all the furniture before letting the truck go on its way.

If you do find a problem, refuse to accept a damaged piece, make sure that you subtract that amount from your total bill, and insist that it be returned to the company. This must be for a legitimate reason that you can clearly state on the invoice such as a stain on the fabric, damage to the wood, wrong item shipped, or that substitutions were expressly forbidden.

Resources

BOOKS

You should be able to find the following books at www.Amazon. com.

If you like vintage furniture (let's not call it used), try one of Rachel Ashwell *Shabby Chic* books on how to decorate elegantly and for a lot less money. Amazon lists four books in all. Here is one.

> *Rachel Ashwell's Shabby Chic: Treasure Hunting & Decorating Guide* by Rachel Ashwell, $35.00, Regan Books, 1998.

INTERNET

I have created an updated and comprehensive list of useful furniture web sites at the web page for this book at:

www.savvydiscounts.com/thebook

North Carolina is known for its decades of furniture design and manufacturing. Over 60% of all furniture manufactured in the U.S. is made within a 200 mile radius of central North Carolina. This North Carolina furniture web site has comprehensive information and links.

www.ncfurnitureonline.com

Links to quality manufacturers:

www.americandrew.com	*www.hancockandmoore.com*
www.bakerfurniture.com	*www.hickorychair.com*
www.barcalounger.com	*www.lanefurniture.com*
www.bernhardtfurniture.com	*www.pearsoncompany.com*
www.broyhillfurn.com	*www.sealyfurniture.com*
www.centuryfurniture.com	*www.thomasville.com*
www.drexelheritage.com	*www.veryvanguard.com*

Ready to assemble furniture:

www.ikea-usa.com

Versatile, changeable futons:

www.thefutonshop.com

Read the online furniture guide and browse the furniture online:

www.pier1.com

Try these office supply stores with catalogues and excellent web sites. Some list clearance furniture, have a general clearance center and an online rebate center:

www.officedepot.com

www.officemax.com

www.quillcorp.com

www.staples.com

www.viking.com

A library of online furniture guides, search by brand or piece, and view a buyers guide:

www.furnitureguide.com

The Federal Trade Commission (FTC) guides for the Household Furniture Industry:

www.ftc.gov/bcp/guides/furniture-gd.htm

"Your Most Complete & Project Marketplace"; detailed information about kit furniture:

www.kitguy.com/cat_furniture.asp

To read reviews or find comments:

www.reviewboard.com

www.planetfeedback.com

Search the archives of newsgroups for letters relating to service or product reliability:

groups.google.com

You can also post questions on the appropriate newsgroup.
To check if there have been any unresolved complaints with a dealer go to the Better Business Bureau site:

www.bbb.com

Gems, Jewelry and Phony Discounts

All That Glitters Is Not Gold

Overview

Jewelry can be a particularly emotional purchase. Jewelry is more than just the stones and the metal. I know this because my wife is a jeweler and I can see the comfort that many people get from her well-made art.

Now consider an engagement ring or wedding ring. Such a piece of jewelry, no matter what the cost, has a meaning separate from the precious gem involved. When the bride sees the ring she must have, what couple is going to engage in hard bargaining and careful scrutiny?

Emotions aside, jewelry is a particularly tricky purchase. I suspect that there is much more deception than the number of consumer complaints would suggest. The reason is that many people do not know they have been taken. According to a CBS News survey about 30% of 10 karat gold was less than 10 karats. Yet how many people are going to check? According to one estimate, roughly 10% of diamonds have been enhanced and sold as quality stones. Yet only a well-trained gemologist with the right equipment can tell the difference between an enhanced diamond and a natural stone. Numerous television reports have shown that unscrupulous jewelers may try to pass off lower quality gems as top of the line. Laboratory-created gems might be confused with naturally mined stones. Plus there are imitations as well.

I am sorry to rain on your parade, but there are many pitfalls involved with jewelry. The reason for this is that only an expert can accurately judge the value of a gemstone and only an experienced buyer can be certain that a gold chain with a gold clasp is the grade of gold the seller claims it to be.

However, when you do buy a genuine quality diamond ring or gold chain, you have bought an item that ought to hold its value for the time you own it. Naturally the price of all gems and precious metals will fluctuate with the market, yet unlike most other products covered in this book, jewelry can keep an intrinsic value and could even be worth more in ten or twenty years. For example, a $1,000 computer bought in 1990 has completely depreciated and is now virtually worthless. However, a $1,000 necklace bought at the same time could still be worth about $1,000 as long as it has been properly cleaned and maintained.

What Buyers Need to Know

With jewelry being such a heartfelt purchase, it may seem odd to get super technical. Yet to make sure you are getting a worthwhile purchase, one that is what it purports to be, you need to get specific. This is the only way you can be certain that you are getting a gem that is worth the price you are paying.

The following system is used for grading gemstones:

Known as the four C's they are: color, clarity, cut, and carat weight.

Color: refers to the strength of the color for a particular kind of stone. Gemologists grade diamonds on a scale from D, being the whitest, to Z, very brown or yellow. There are several scales which add to the confusion. When getting an appraisal, have the appraiser state which scale was used.

Clarity: As we have pointed out, gems are made by nature and not by humans. So it is natural in the process of being created that there are flaws. All stones will have what are called inclusions or imperfections. Since no stone is ever flawless, the Federal Trade Commission states that a diamond can only be labeled as "flawless" when no inclusions can be seen under a 10 times magnification.

Cut: Cut describes the general shape of the stone and the facets, the small flat planes, that shape the finished stone. It also refers to size, angle, uniformity, and polish of the facets.

Carat: Carat is a weight measurement. One carat weighs 200 milligrams. There are 100 points to a carat. Dealers often round off the carat weight so a .41 carat could have a weight between .405 and .414. Since carat refers to weight, always ask how much a gem weighs not how large it is. Some jewelers will say that a stone "spreads one carat" which does not mean it weighs one carat but only looks like a one-carat stone.

Other Terms:

Clarity-enhanced or fracture-filled gemstones: artificially treated gemstones including diamonds, rubies, and emeralds which look like expensive stones but in fact are often poor quality. As long as these are labeled properly these gems might be a good deal. Yet they are often sold as high quality to unsuspecting customers. If you own one of these, it must be handled very differently from a regular stone. Heat from a jewelers torch will reveal cracks that the treatment covered up. As if this weren't enough, many professional jewelers have trouble identifying a treated stone.

Gemstone treatments: According to the Federal Trade Commission, treatments "such as heating, dyeing or bleaching—can improve a stone's appearance or durability. Some treatments are permanent; some may create special care requirement. Treatments may also affect the stone's value."

Synthetic gemstone or laboratory-created gem: This is the same chemically as a natural stone, but made by humans.

Imitation gemstone: This looks like a natural gemstone but is not the same chemically.

Pearls:

Cultured pearls: Grown by humans in oysters.

No Gem Is Flawless

Gemstones and pearls are made by nature. All stones are flawed. Unlike any other purchase in this book, gemstones, except for artificial ones, are not manufactured and not the perfect products that we expect from other products covered in this book.

Imitation or simulated pearls: Must be labeled as such and are made from any number of processes.

Natural: Natural pearls are made accidentally in oysters and are quite rare.

Pearls are judged according to their size, luster, shape, and color. There is quite a variety. A necklace of 50 pearls with the same sized cultured pearls could be worth as little as $50 or as much as $1,000.

Now to thoroughly confuse you:

Gold-filled or gold-plated: a thin covering on another metal.

Karat: (not to be confused with carat) a measurement that indicates how much gold is in a particular item. 24 karats is pure gold but is not normally available because it is too soft. Therefore gold alloys are common. For example, a 14-karat gold chain will contain 14 parts gold and 10 parts alloy metal. Only metal with 10k or more can be labeled as gold in the U.S.A. The karats and manufacturers trademark must be stamped on the jewelry.

Solid gold: means that the gold is 10k or higher and does not have a hollow center.

Sterling silver: contains 92.5% silver and 7.5% copper.

Before Shopping

The more expensive the jewelry, the more careful you should be. This can be particularly difficult with an engagement or wedding ring. In spite of deadlines and hot-blooded emotions, my advice still holds true. No bride wants to be given a beautiful large diamond ring only to find months later that it is enhanced and worth almost nothing.

Decide roughly what you want to buy and how much you want to spend. Set an absolute upper limit on your budget. That way you can't be talked into buying just a slightly better ring. You might get more for your money with emeralds, sapphires, and rubies, so consider these as well. If your new jewelry must go with an outfit, you should wear that clothing when you go shopping.

Comparison Shopping

You are not only shopping for specific jewelry, you are shopping for a reputable jeweler who carries rings and necklaces in styles that you like. Before buying from any store you should check with the Better Business Bureau and the Jewelers Vigilance Committee (see the Resources section at the end of this chapter) for any complaints. Ask to see the jeweler's accreditation. There should be framed certificates from national jewelry associations on the wall of the shop. Look for a store that has been in business for twenty years. Ask your friends and family who wear jewelry that you admire about the stores they patronize.

Never shop at a store that will not let you return the jewelry within a reasonable amount of time for a full refund. If you are giving a gift, the store should allow a return if the piece does not fit.

Since jewelry is worn, you might need to adjust the fit. Pick a store that will do modifications if necessary. Ask about any charges involved.

Because there are so many variables, it is hard to compare one ring to another or one necklace to another. Yet after shopping around, you should begin to get a clear idea of what a diamond ring will cost and which reputable dealer offers the best bargain.

Buyer Beware

There are dozens of ways to get fooled when you buy jewelry. Here are detailed warnings. While gold items must be marked with a stamp stating the number of karats, they also must by law be stamped with the trademark of the manufacturer. If you see a karat stamp but no trademark, this is a red flag. My advice is simple. Do not buy this gold product.

Next you could be told that a gold necklace is 14 karat gold. When you question the sellers, they point to a 14 karat gold stamp with the manufacturers trademark, as required by U.S. law on the clasp. So it's 14 karats right? Wrong! The clasp is different from the necklace itself, which must have its own karat and manufacturer's trademark stamp.

And then there are those sales. Have you even wondered why jewelry often goes on sale around Mother's Day? Other types of businesses would charge top dollar during these periods of high demand. Who would have a genuine sale weeks before Christmas? So why does jewelry go on sale just when you are thinking about buying a Valentine's gift for your wife? Several investigations found that the regular prices were inflated and that the jewelry sold only briefly, if ever, at that price. In short the discounts are often bogus.

I have pointed out that even experienced jewelers can be fooled by treatments such as clarity-enhanced or fracture-filled gemstones. Since there are so many floating around you could buy one without realizing it. Avoid stores with no prices on the jewelry. Pushy salespeople will try to steer you toward the more costly stuff before you have had a chance to look at the less expensive gems.

Get an independent appraisal for an expensive piece. Some jewelers can give you a gem report from a separate gemological lab. A licensed appraiser can give you an educated opinion about the value of an antique piece or a new piece you are thinking of buying. Since appraisals are subjective, they might vary as much as 10%. This is to be expected. Appraisers should be licensed by an accredited gemologist association. Pay an appraiser by the hour, not as a percent of the piece. Ask beforehand about estimated costs. Never get an appraisal from an appraiser recommended by the jewelry store; he or she could be working hand-in-hand with that store.

To read more in detail about accepted and deceptive jewelry practices see the Resources section at the end of this chapter.

Discount Strategies

Best Single Strategy
Basic Comparison Shopping

With basic comparison shopping of reputable local dealers, you should be able to locate the lowest retail price for jewelry that is within your price range and of the quality that you require.

1. Comparison shopping

This is the best single strategy for getting a great deal. Please read about this in more detail at the top of this Discount Strategies section.

2. Haggling for a low price

New jewelry has a substantial markup so haggle away. While chain stores may not want to bargain, independent stores may be more open.

3. Haggling for extras

Ask for a couple of years worth of cleaning with your purchase. If you buy pearls, ask them to throw in the first restringing for free.

4. Custom configurations

Independent reputable jewelers can make a ring in just about any configuration. This could save money and be more to your liking since you can create your own look. A custom order requires that you work with the jeweler on the design and that you understand how jewelry can be created.

5. Regular sales

May.

6. Rebates

While you may see occasional rebates, they are not common for jewelry.

7. Unusual discounts and sales

While I have warned you against confusing a treated or fracture-filled gemstone for the real thing, buying an enhanced stone for a reasonable price could be a very good deal. If you have a limited budget, no one will know, without a microscope, that the huge diamond you are wearing, has been treated.

8. Internet shopping and mail order

Because these stores do not have the overhead of a brick-and-mortar shop, you might be able to find significant discounts. Everything that I mentioned about checking the dealer's reputation and getting a detailed invoice, applies double to mail order and the Internet. I would not deal with firms that only have a post office box and not a physical address. I would also make sure that the firm had a telephone number and that a real live person answered that phone.

9. Outlet stores and outlet malls

Avoid this kind of jewelry store. Wholesale stores, kiosks, and street vendors often sell jewelry at cut-rate prices. Most of the time these are not good deals and the jewelry is often misrepresented.

10. Closeouts and discontinued models

Styles come and go so you might be able to find an outgoing style that the store will let go for a song.

11. Floor models, demonstrators, scratch-and-dent, blemished, seconds

This does not apply to this category.

Discount Wedding Bands

When two friends of mine were getting married, they looked around for wedding bands. They were able to buy matching rings that were being discontinued. They bought the samples for that design at a much lower price.

12. Refurbished

This does not apply to this category.

13. Used

Never buy antique jewelry on your own unless you are an expert. It is easy to be fooled. Expensive purchases should be appraised first. However, if you are knowledgeable, you could find some excellent bargains.

14. Financing

Avoid store credit which can be over 20%. A low-interest credit card might be the best way to go, if you make a regular payment each month for the same amount. If you are offered a no interest or no payments deal for 6 to 12 months, ask for a discount if you pay cash.

15. Extra discounts

If you are buying a substantial piece, ask the store to throw in a quality jewelry box so that you can store your jewelry properly.

Example of combined discounts:

Haggle for your very best price on a necklace (1st discount) and then offer to buy the matching earrings (2nd discount) for a substantial discount.

Making the Deal

Some diamonds may come with a certificate which gives a full description. If a certificate is not available, you should get an invoice. This is the only way to be certain that you have bought what you thought you bought and be able to correct the situation if there is a problem. Get all those technical specifications in writing on an official invoice form from the jeweler. The jeweler should state specifically the 4 Cs for a gemstone and the composition of the metal for the stone's setting. He should also state whether the stone was naturally mined, laboratory-created, or is an imitation. If the stone is treated, the invoice should state how it has been treated and if the treatment is permanent. In addition, a drawing, a close-up photograph, or a description might also be added showing the cut and inclusions. Include anything else in writing on the invoice that you were told verbally. A mention or copy of the return policy should be referenced.

After the Sale

If the jewelry is expensive, I would have it appraised by at least one independent appraiser soon after the sale. Do not tell him or her how much you paid or where you got it. Have him or her write down the appraisal before you show your invoice from the store. If the discrepancy is more than 10%, you should return the jewelry with a written opinion from the appraiser.

Bear in mind that there will be some differences of opinion. One person might rate a diamond as having an E when it comes to color and another might say F. Small differences like these should be tolerated. Also keep in mind that what you pay for jewelry retail will be different from what it is worth if you tried to sell it to a dealer. But if you paid $5,000 and an appraiser says that it is worth only $1,000, there is a problem.

Expensive jewelry should be insured. You may be able to add a floater policy to your homeowners policy that covers your jewelry. You should get an appraisal that you can use to back up any insurance claim. You can insure it for the replacement cost which is the price to replace the piece. Or you can insure it for the estate value which is the price the piece would bring on the open market and less than the replacement cost. Jewelry can be insured for loss, or theft, or damage or all three in an "all risk" policy.

Jewelry needs to be handled properly to keep its value. If a set of instructions comes with that string of pearls, read them. Pearls, in particular, need to be handled carefully. For example, you should never add perfume, cosmetics, or hairspray while wearing pearls. Do these first and then put on that strand of pearls. Pearls can scratch easily so handle them carefully and store them in tissue or a chamois bag. Pearls should be restrung once a year. Avoid wearing rings when doing harsh cleaning or using household chemicals. Avoid chlorine especially with gold—and this includes chlorinated swimming pools.

Resources

BOOKS
You should be able to find the following books at www.Amazon. com.

> *Gemstones of the World, Revised Edition,* by Walter Schumann, $24.95, Sterling Publications, 2000.

> *Jewelry & Gems: The Buying Guide—How to Buy Diamonds, Pearls, Colored Gemstones, Gold & Jewelry With Confidence and Knowledge (5th Edition)* by Antoinette Matlins and A. C. Bonanno, $24.95, Gemstone Press, 2001.

Smart Questions for Savvy Shoppers: The Guide That Gets You the Most for Your Dollar, by Dorothy Leeds with Sharyn Kolberg, $8.99, HarperPaperbacks, 1994.

INTERNET

I have created an updated and comprehensive list of useful jewelry web sites at the web page for this book at:

www.savvydiscounts.com/thebook

From the Federal Trade Commission (FTC): These guides are surprisingly clear, well written and simple to skim.
Guides for the Jewelry, Precious Metals, and Pewter Industries:

www.ftc.gov/bcp/guides/jewel-gd.htm

Beloved . . . Bejeweled . . . Be Careful! What to Know Before You Buy Jewelry:

www.ftc.gov/bcp/conline/pubs/alerts/jewelweb.htm

Buying Gold and Gemstone Jewelry: The Heart of the Matter:

www.ftc.gov/bcp/conline/pubs/alerts/goldalrt.htm

The Jewelers Vigilance Committee (JVC), since 1912, is a not-for-profit trade association whose mission is to maintain the jewelry industry's highest ethical standards:

www.jvclegal.org

Jewelers of America is the largest trade organization for retail jewelers, with more than 10,000 members nationwide. Members must adhere to a set of ethics. Use this site to find a member jeweler near you:

www.jewelers.org

This About site is quite extensive; it includes a buyers guide and advice for savvy shoppers:

jewelry.about.com

Well-known retail jewelers online:

www.friedmans.com

www.kay.com

www.tiffany.com

www.zales.com

Search the archives of newsgroups for letters relating to service or product reliability:

groups.google.com

You can also post questions on the appropriate newsgroup.
To check if there have been any unresolved complaints with a dealer go to the Better Business Bureau site:

www.bbb.com

Internet Research and Shopping Plus Mail Order

Window-Shop with Your Web Browser

Web Research

The Internet is a window-shopper's paradise. It is an excellent place to start when you want to learn about technical terms, manufacturer specific terms, various features, and available rebates. Treat it as an educational tool that will give you what you need to know.

You can read about two different digital cameras then print out and compare specification sheets. You can check the various newsgroups for unsolicited opinions from real people. You can research problems with the company's rebate programs. In addition, you can get an accurate sense of how much you should pay. You can do all of this in the privacy of your home and away from all the sales pressure you will encounter once you walk into a showroom.

How to Find What You Want

Part of the art of using the Internet is knowing how to search. This is true whether you are using a sophisticated search engine such as Google.com or a site specific search engine that will search only that site and may not have as many features. A good rule of thumb is to list several specific words that you want on the pages brought up by the search. It also helps if you put the most important words first, then the next most important, and so on. While it won't be a great English sentence, it will be in a form that a computer search engine can understand.

Let's say I want to find the spec sheet for a Sony camera. If I only look for just the word "Sony" it would bring up thousands of sites that sell Sony products. If I now look for the words "digital camera Sony," it will bring up fewer sites, but again Sony is sold by lots of retailers and has lots of digital cameras. Now if I add the model number: "digital camera Sony CD1000" it will limit the search to just that camera, but again many listings of stores that carry that model. Finally if I type in the words: "digital camera Sony CD1000 specifications" it will take me directly to a site with the specifications for that camera.

Let's take another example. Suppose you wanted to buy a

How Do You Know If a Used Price Is Okay?

ABC News aired a report about how pawnbrokers could know the fair market value of the wide variety of used items that they are asked to buy. It was simple. They looked on eBay. With literally millions of items for sale, they could check and be certain that they could recover their money if necessary. So if the pros do it, you should too.

A Store to Avoid

As always, the Internet shopper's credo should be "buyer beware" which is as true today as it was in ancient Rome. Watch your wallet. I found that one company kept appearing at the top of the digital camera list with consistently the lowest prices. I called to discover that the camera I wanted was not in stock at that time. Another call about a different camera resulted in the same answer. Something did not smell right. So I went to the newsgroup archive and typed in the name of the retail company. Lo and behold, dozens of angry letters appeared from customers who had been promised merchandise months ago, but had received nothing. Clearly this was a company to avoid.

late-model Ford Taurus but wanted to find out if there were any repair problems. In a test I went to the Google.com advanced search and asked it to find pages with all the words "repair history" but these words did not have to be together. I also told it to find the exact phrase "2000 Ford Taurus." This search brought up about 40 relevant sites which were enough to find good information, but not so many that I was overwhelmed.

If you are buying a standard item, you should check the manufacturer's web site for a description and full list of specifications which will generally be much more extensive than you will find on the pages of an online retail store that sells that same item. For example, the Sony site for U.S. customers will often have more detailed information about a camera than a retailer who sells that Sony product.

Be aware that many companies are now multinational. Normally the web address (URL) for a company will be: www.

companyname.com. Make sure when you get the resulting page that you are at the U.S. site or click to go to the U.S. site.

If you are buying used, you can check current used prices on eBay. I suggest that you check several sales, not just one, if possible, as I have seen the same item sell for $300 and $400. What you find on eBay will be a rough guideline, but still an accurate one, because it shows you the exact price that a willing buyer and a willing seller agreed on.

To find what something has sold for on eBay, go to: www.ebay.com. Click on "Search," then click on "Completed items." Next type in the item you want to look for in the Search box. Be as specific as possible. If the search yields too few results, make it a little less specific. If you get too many results, make your search more specific.

There are a number of comparison-shopping sites on the Internet. Many of these offer ratings and reviews and allow you

Finding the Best Online Store

Several years ago I was comparison shopping on the Web with an online shopping service. I was looking for a Toshiba computer. I found a number of good deals. Yet once I compared shipping prices, return policies, and the star ratings for customer satisfaction, the deal was not so great. In addition I insisted that there be a toll-free 800 number where I could call a real person and get intelligent answers. After much searching I ended up with one of my favorite stores, CDW. It did not have the best price, although it was a good price, but had the lowest shipping. Since I knew CDW's reputation, I was confident that I would be satisfied. And I was.

to rearrange the listings by categories such as price. Initially the top listings may be companies that have paid to be listed. See the Resources section at the end of this chapter for web addresses.

You can even look for the best price on a new car within a specific mile radius from your home. Naturally if you find a tempting deal, you should check out the dealer's reputation on the Internet as well. This is especially true if the dealer is many miles from you, since you may be working with that dealer if problems arise.

Newsgroups or discussion groups are especially valuable. While it will take you a while to wade through all the messages, you will be reading real reports from real people who either love a product or have had problems. On the Internet people rarely spare harsh words when they feel that they have been taken or been given shoddy treatment by a company. See the Resources section at the end of this chapter for web addresses.

The reputation of the company, or dealer or individual you are buying from on the Internet is critical. Always check a dealer's rating on eBay and read comments from buyers. I would not automatically avoid a seller who had one complaint lodged against him or her, since that complaint could just as easily be the buyer's fault. However, I would definitely avoid a seller with three or more complaints. This means the seller is doing something wrong.

There are a number of ways to check the reputation of a business from a simple "star" rating at price comparison sites, to the Better Business Bureau, to individual messages posted on newsgroups. Avoid new businesses without a track record. On the Internet, it is very easy for a person or company to pretend to be something it is not. Never do business with a company that does not have a physical address and a toll-free number. The more money you plan to spend, the more careful you should be.

Suggested Search Words

The Internet is always changing. Old addresses may no longer work and new companies may become major Internet sites. To see the latest web offerings do a periodic search. The following key words and suggestions should help you locate current online stores and research material for the products mentioned in this book.

For searches, I highly recommend www.google.com which is a very fast and accurate search engine. It also allows advanced searches which can, for example, exclude certain words or certain sites.

For Internet stores, I would include the words *online sales,* since just the word *sales* will bring up brick-and-mortar retail stores in addition to businesses that sell on the Web.

When looking for a product, be specific: brand name, category, and model number are usually necessary, such as "Sony digital camera CD1000." If you are looking for closeouts and refurbished items, you might include most of the words mentioned above such as *online sales closeouts Sony digital camera.* If a search does not bring up enough web sites to choose from, then broaden your search by eliminating a word or two. If the search brings up too many web sites, then add a word or two. The best site for your needs is often not among the top listed, but farther down the search results or it could even be on the next page. Computers and search engines are only so good; you have to decide which link is the most appropriate.

What To Buy on the Internet or Through Mail Order

The Internet will be useful for buying many products covered in this book. Generally speaking, however, I would avoid buying these items directly off the Internet:

New and used cars

A new or used appliance unless you can order from a local store

Jewelry

Cars really need to be seen and inspected in a hands-on purchase, shipping a faulty appliance back to a warehouse would be a major hassle, and with jewelry the problems with deception are even greater than through a retail dealer.

Under some circumstances the following might be bought on the Internet from a reputable dealer. Before you go ahead and plunk down cash, however, make sure you read my advice about how to order on the Internet later in this chapter.

Audiovisual equipment

Computers

Exercise equipment—new and used.

A lot of new equipment is sold directly by companies to consumers on the Internet, such as that by NordicTrack. This might be the best way to buy new since you will be dealing directly with the manufacturer. Because the price of used exercise equipment is dramatically lower than that of new, it might be worth your while to check out what you can find on eBay.

Audiovisual equipment

If you know exactly what you want and understand all the specifications, buying on the Internet might be okay. For the less knowledgeable, I recommend a store, even with annoying salespeople, because then you can see what you are buying.

197

Computers

If you are buying a standard configuration, many of the online dealers such as Dell or Gateway have a good reputation for quality, customer service, and customer support. The less standard your configuration, the better off you might be with a local technician who can build a custom computer just for you.

Furniture

If you are going to special order furniture, you might as well get it from a reputable online discount dealer and wait for delivery rather than from an expensive local dealer and wait for delivery. It will probably take the same amount of time in both cases.

How to Order

General Advice for Mail Order and Online Companies

Mail order and Internet firms can be an excellent way to get the best deal. Many companies offer the very lowest price on a number of items. They also offer you a range of selection that cannot be matched by virtually any local store. For example, there is no brick-and-mortar store which carries as many books and is as big as Amazon.com.

Getting anything shipped to you has severe limitations. It can cost you much more money in the long run and be much more troublesome than buying close to where you live. For example, returns are time-consuming, expensive, and require precise paperwork. Not only will you pay for the return shipping, you must also insure it. Many firms now charge a restocking fee for returned merchandise that is not defective. In addition, the initial cost of shipping and handling will not be refunded.

The trick is that you need to know exactly what you want, the make, model, color, etc. You can determine this by going into local retail stores to look at merchandise. You should take a notepad with you and write down specifics, such as the extras that are included in the standard package as shipped by the manufacturer.

After looking at the real item in a store, you can follow up by going to the manufacturer's web site. Print out a general description plus the specifications page. It is unlikely that a salesperson at the retail store would understand all the capabilities of that digital camera you are thinking of buying, and specific questions such as how pictures are transferred to the computer will be answered better in detail at the manufacturer's site.

Before you order you should understand the policy about the following: How many days are allowed for a refund or exchange? Must you get an authorization before returns and if so how is this done? Is there a restocking fee and how much is it? Is shipping refunded or only the price of the item?

As we noted in the Introduction, you should *never* fill out the warranty card before the return date has passed. Most stores will not let you send back an item if that card has been written on.

Delivery with mail order is a bit of a hassle. The item is often shipped in a bigger box which must be opened first before the product box can be examined. You will have to do this quickly because the UPS or other delivery person may be waiting at the door, impatient for you to sign. While this may sound like a lot of trouble, the extra effort is definitely worth it. If you follow the necessary steps as outlined in this book, you will end up a satisfied customer.

Ordering Off the Web

At the moment consumers may not have to pay taxes for items purchased entirely over the Internet from an out-of-state firm. However, the shipping charge often cancels out any tax savings. With the advanced technology of the Internet, it would seem that you could make a purchase directly online and that there would be few problems. However, I have found that there are consistent problems. For example, out of five orders I made online during a three-month period, only one went through without any glitch.

A simple rule of thumb is this: If the purchase you are making is expensive, important, or must reach you quickly, you should pick up the phone and place the order the old-fashioned way. In any case there should be an 800 number you can call if there is a problem with your order. When you order online, all kinds of things can happen. Just recently I placed an order for a small item which seemed to go through, but then the site crashed and I could not find out for six hours if the order had actually been received. I did not want to place the order again, because that would mean the possibility of duplicate orders and then the hassle of getting a refund, so I was stuck. Fortunately it was a small unimportant order. Imagine my frustration level if it had been an expensive and important order.

No one is accountable for an Internet order if things go wrong. If you are counting on a rapid response to e-mail, don't hold your breath. Companies that promise quick quality customer service can take days to get back to you. And frankly, e-mail does not work well if you have more than a simple request or you need to ask follow-up questions.

With the phone you have an individual who is responsible for your order, who you can talk to, and who will answer questions. To take advantage of all this good stuff, you should write down the person's name and the time and date you talked so that if there is a problem, you can follow up.

If you do decide to order directly off the Internet, you should print the page confirming your order. This is essential. It will contain the order number and the items ordered and will be vital in case of any problems.

Naturally ordering off eBay is different since it is an online auction. If it is an expensive item, you should call the dealer if there is a number listed. At the very least you should send the dealer an e-mail. Getting a quick accurate response is a good indicator that the dealer is reliable.

At the end of this chapter I have created a form with essential questions you should ask. When you buy off the Internet or through a mail-order firm, you should copy this page and fill it out for each order. As I have suggested, use the phone if the order is expensive or important.

Use a Credit Card

I recommend that you use a credit card with Internet and mail-order firms. Using a credit card may give you certain rights to dispute a purchase if you have a problem. This is especially useful when you are ordering at a distance. While there are a number of options now through PayPal such as a direct withdrawal from your checking account, I think a credit card is the best choice.

Watch Those S&H Charges

While ordering over the Internet may get you a substantial discount and perhaps save you taxes, you will have to pay shipping. Unfortunately this fee varies widely. It can be only what a carrier such as UPS or Federal Express charges to ship or an inflated charge that includes "handling." I have seen the handling charge almost double the shipping for the same computer when ordered from different retail companies. Since shipping and handling are not refundable, you will lose this amount in case you need to return the product. You would be better off paying more for a computer and less for shipping and handling if the total amount is almost the same.

Resources

I have created an updated and comprehensive list of useful web sites at the web page for this book at:

www.savvydiscounts.com/thebook

For most major companies you simply can put www. in front of the company name followed by .com. Keep in mind that many companies are international so that you may have to navigate from the initial site to the U.S. site:

www.companyname.com

PRICE COMPARISONS

For online price comparisons try these major web sites. Keep in mind that some businesses that have paid for a listing may automatically appear at the top initially. Most services will allow you to rearrange the list for your own purposes:

shopping.yahoo.com

www.BizRate.com

www.Cnet.com

www.Dealtime.com

www.PriceGrabber.com

REVIEWS, FEEDBACK, OPINIONS, COMPLAINTS

To read other peoples opinions or file a complaint of your own go to PlanetFeedback:

www.planetfeedback.com

For reviews of various products:

www.consumerreview.com

www.consumersearch.com

www.epinions.com

www.ratings.net

www.reviewboard.com

Search the archives of newsgroups for letters relating to service or product reliability:

groups.google.com

You can also post questions on the appropriate newsgroup.

To check if there have been any unresolved complaints with a dealer go to the Better Business Bureau site:

www.bbb.com

Standard Form for Ordering
Over the Internet or Via Mail Order

Copy this and fill it out for each order

Tip: When the product arrives, clip the receipt in the package to this sheet of paper and file in a safe place. If you ordered online, clip a printout of your final order page to this page.

Date: _____

Store: _____

Physical address: _____
_____

Web address: _____
_____

Toll-free number: _____

Customer problem e-mail address:
_____

Person you ordered from: _____

Office where that person is located: _____
_____

Item ordered including model number, color, etc.: _____
_____

Extra information (if necessary):
_____
_____

If an electronic item:

Is it sent in the original box as shipped by the manufacturer? _____

Are all accessories included as specified by the manufacturer? _____

Is it gray market? _____

Does it come with a full normal warranty good in the U.S.A.?_____

In stock?: _____

If not when will it be in stock? _____

Cost of item(s): _____

Cost of shipping: _____

Tax: _____

Handling: _____

Total Cost: _____

Approx. shipping date: _____

How will it be shipped? _____

Method of payment: _____

Credit card used: _____

Credit card not to be charged until back order arrives?

Return policy? _____

Number of days to return: _____

Return date starts from date shipped or date delivered? _____

Restocking fee?_____

How much: _____

Return authorization required? _____

Number/e-mail address to obtain return authorization: _____

Format for return authorization: _____
_____

Different address for returns? _____
_____

204

Index

Page numbers in *italic* indicate forms.